Praise for

Transcendent Beauty

*"**Crystal Andrus** has written a deeply compelling book that will open our eyes and help us all—men included—to embrace and honor the magnificence we already possess—a magnificence that is often overlooked and nearly forgotten, yet nonetheless is just waiting for us to uncover it."*

— **Debbie Ford**, the best-selling author of *The Dark Side of the Light Chasers* and *The Best Year of Your Life*

*"**Transcendent Beauty** elevates us to embrace the feminine fullness and strength of mind, body, and spirit, ever reminding us that true beauty is about loving and respecting the 'skin you're in.' It's beautifully written—a must-read for all modern women!"*

— **Colette Baron-Reid**, international intuitive counselor and author of *Remembering the Future*

*"**Transcendent Beauty** gently guides us into the next era of feminism, giving women everywhere the permission we all need to feel beautiful, on the inside and out!"*

— **Caroline Sutherland**, medical intuitive, and the best-selling author of *The Body "Knows"*

Transcendent Beauty

Also by Crystal Andrus

Simply . . . Woman! *The 12-Week Body-Mind-Soul Total Transformation Program*

Hay House Titles of Related Interest

Books

The Body "Knows": *How to Tune in to Your Body and Improve Your Health,* by Caroline Sutherland, Medical Intuitive

Confidence: *Finding It and Living It,* by Barbara De Angelis, Ph.D.

Inspiration: *Your Ultimate Calling,* by Dr. Wayne W. Dyer

Remembering the Future: *The Path to Recovering Intuition,* by Colette Baron-Reid

Secrets & Mysteries: *The Glory and Pleasure of Being a Woman,* by Denise Linn

Trust Your Vibes: *Secret Tools for Six-Sensory Living,* by Sonia Choquette

A Very Hungry Girl: *How I Filled Up On Life . . . and How You Can Too!* by Jessica Weiner

The Way of the Belly: *8 Essential Secrets of Beauty, Sensuality, Health, Happiness, and Outrageous Fun,* by Neena & Veena, with Nancy Bruning

Card Decks and Kit

The Best Year of Your Life Kit, by Debbie Ford

Goddess Guidance Oracle Cards, by Doreen Virtue, Ph.D.

Mind/Body Makeover Cards, by Mona Lisa Schulz, M.D., Ph.D.

All of the above are available at your local bookstore, or may be ordered by visiting:

Hay House USA: **www.hayhouse.com®**
Hay House Australia: **www.hayhouse.com.au**
Hay House UK: **www.hayhouse.co.uk**
Hay House South Africa: **orders@psdprom.co.za**
Hay House India: **www.hayhouseindia.co.in**

It Begins with a Single Choice . . . to Be!

Crystal Andrus

HAY HOUSE, INC.
Carlsbad, California
London • Sydney • Johannesburg
Vancouver • Hong Kong • Mumbai

Published and distributed in the United States by: Hay House, Inc.: www.hayhouse.com • ***Published and distributed in Australia by:*** Hay House Australia Pty. Ltd.: www.hayhouse.com.au • ***Published and distributed in the United Kingdom by:*** Hay House UK, Ltd.: www.hayhouse.co.uk • ***Published and distributed in the Republic of South Africa by:*** Hay House SA (Pty), Ltd.: orders@psdprom.co.za • ***Distributed in Canada by:*** Raincoast: www.raincoast.com • ***Published in India by:*** Hay House Publications (India) Pvt. Ltd.: www.hayhouseindia.co.in • ***Distributed in India by:*** Media Star: booksdivision@mediastar.co.in

Editorial supervision: Jill Kramer • *Design:* Amy Gingery

Library of Congress Cataloging-in-Publication Data

Andrus, Crystal.
Transcendent beauty : it begins with a single choice . . . to be! / Crystal Andrus.
p. cm.
ISBN-13: 978-1-4019-0679-5 (tradepaper)
ISBN-10: 1-4019-0679-6 (tradepaper)
1. Beauty, Personal--Psychological aspects. I. Title.
RA778.A539 2006
646.7'042--dc22
2005033543

ISBN 13: 978-1-4019-0679-5
ISBN 10: 1-4019-0679-6

09 08 07 06 4 3 2 1
1st printing, March 2006

Printed in the United States of America

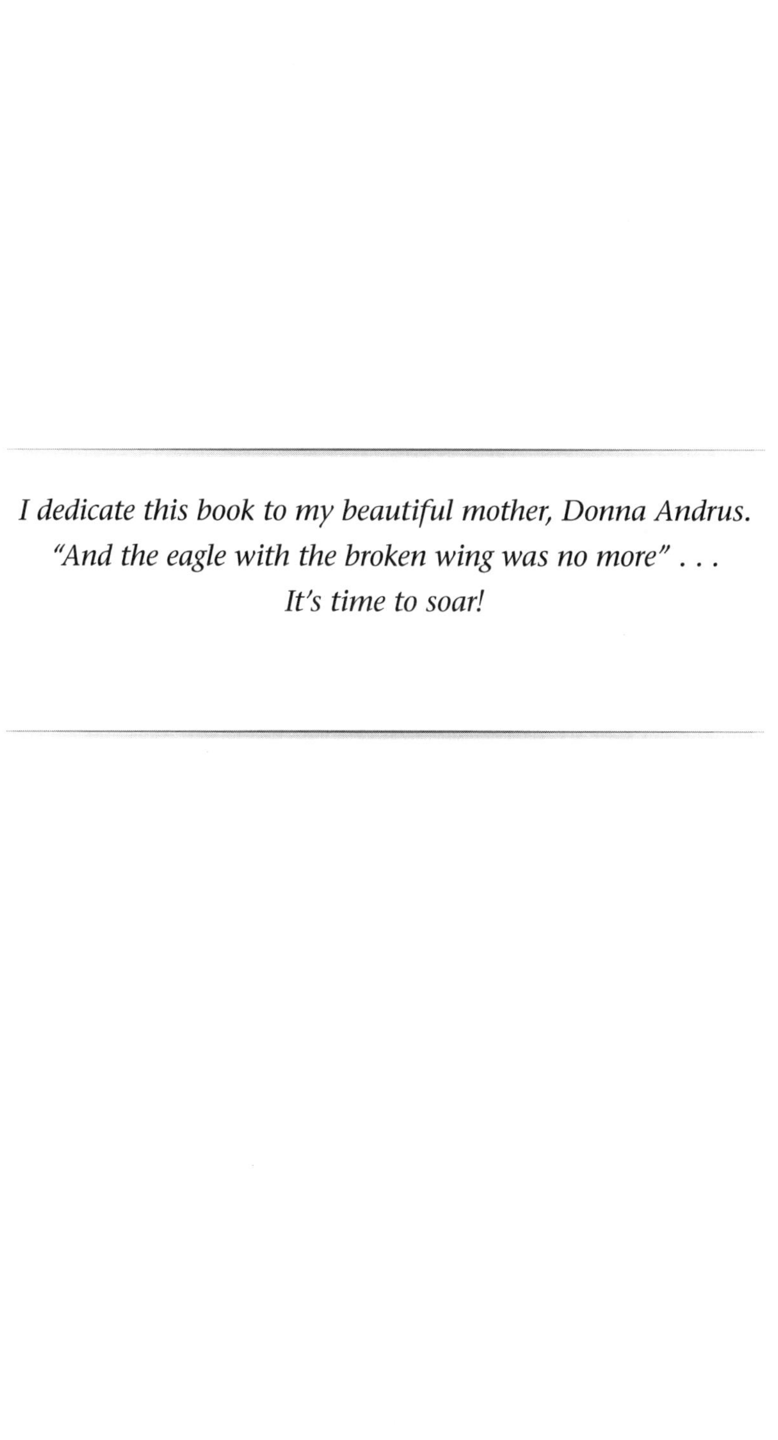

I dedicate this book to my beautiful mother, Donna Andrus.
"And the eagle with the broken wing was no more" . . .
It's time to soar!

Contents

The Eagle's Broken Wing

by Donna Andrus

She sat alone, lame, in stillness and silence . . .
Looking out at a world filled with foggy images.
She saw broken rivers and burned bridges,
Pastel shadowed rainbows and sunsets,
Hazy roses opening and closing, without acknowledgment.
So many gray, hollow, disappointments!
She felt very sad.
Yet she sat proud and strong,
On the highest peak . . .
At the crest of happiness.
And the clouds and moon caressed her.
And the stars twinkled promise!
She could not remember how she got here,
But she knew she was home.
So she heaved gratitude and curled up reclusive . . .
And hid her head beneath her broken wing.
She could not fly!
Not until she healed!
Would she ever?
She thought about the mountains she had soared over . . .
The tribulations she had endured.
The dark storms she had traveled through,
Inside clouds packed with failure.
But still she had plundered on to protect her family . . .
In order to survive.
But oh my, how the fox had tricked her!
And now her feathers were tattered and battered,
And she was broken and alone!
No matter how hard she wished or how hard she tried,
She could not fly . . . yet she was an eagle strong!
What terrible shame she felt.
So she hid her head beneath her broken wing . . .

And finally she fell asleep!
When she awoke the sun was rising.
She fluttered herself, sighing wearily,
Remembering . . . she was the eagle mother.
Looking over the horizon, she saw her son,
Soaring amongst a pink and purple sky.
And her daughters collecting food,
To feed their families.
She saw all was well!
Still she felt anguished!
Could they survive without her?
And how could she survive without them . . .
With a broken wing?
Crushed and tired, she shook her broken feathers.
Then closing weary eyes, she prayed for courage and strength . . .
Way beneath her broken spirit.
When the sun rose again, she breathed fresh morning air,
And something wonderful had happened.
Miraculously, she lifted her wings in harmony,
and dove out beyond . . . into the sunlit horizon.
The time was hers again . . . she knew it!
She directed all her energy into the pink and purple sky,
Where her son soared and her daughters collected food,
And where they all belonged!
She rolled amongst the clouds, smiling . . .
Knowing instinctively how to fly!
She also knew that no matter how bad the wound, everything heals!
And with faith and love, nothing is impossible.
Clasping boldly onto her spirit, she rejoiced,
Then she plunged upwards with joy and frivolity . . .
And the eagle with the broken wing was no more!

Introduction

Beauty begins with a single choice . . . *to be*. Imagine just being beautiful, and having the absolute certainty that you are.

Unfortunately, most of us have bought into the myth that if we try hard enough, we may perhaps . . . eventually . . . sort of . . . feel it. Worrying, stressing, wondering, planning, devising, speculating, and most often doubting, we're constantly searching for "it." But it never comes . . . and it never will, because being beautiful is only attainable with two effortless words: *I am.*

You see, transcendent beauty is a state of being. It can't be bought or bottled, found or lost—it simply *is*. It has no real definition, for it's in everything and everyone. It's found in the gentle slope of a woman's waist as it cascades around her hip while she effortlessly strolls through a crowded room. It's in the twinkle of her eye as she laughs out loud with old friends. It's in the tender touch as she strokes her baby's hair, and is captured in the moment she extends her hand toward her lover with passion.

The transcendently beautiful are brilliantly lit, brimming with bliss, and radiating a splendor that's never ending and enthralling. The aura from these people is not a chaotic, manic type of intense energy with happy peaks and sad valleys; rather, it's a gentle, consistent, and infinite presence. Such individuals don't look to impress others purposefully—yet nevertheless, their radiance is so powerful that the world is naturally attracted to them. They smile effortlessly and love passionately because they know that everything in their life happens with synchronicity and the miraculous is commonplace. They simply *know* that everything—from the way they think, feel, react, eat, speak, move, touch, and love to what they surround themselves with—will either increase their light or dim it. The fact that they shine with an indescribable quality isn't their aim but rather a by-product of the way they live their lives.

You may think that only monks and sages can achieve this state, yet we've all met so-called regular people who exude "joie de vivre" even in the midst of pandemonium. The greatest teachers and healers ooze this magic, and many of us ache for whatever it is they possess. People worldwide are spending billions of dollars hoping to find it in a cream, pill, or potion. They work like mad to buy the best car, fanciest house, and most perfect outfit . . . and then feel disillusioned and hopeless when they wake up in the morning, look in the mirror, and still reject what they see. It seems that these poor souls can never feel good enough.

If you feel like a member of the latter group, take heart! While achieving transcendent beauty is actually quite simple, until now it's been difficult for so many of us to reach because our idealism—or our attachment to the paradigm of beauty—has severed us from ever attaining it. We fret that our looks are biased and competitive and unless we're the "ideal," we'll never be beautiful . . . never feel good about ourselves . . . never shine.

The simple fact is that we women are so exhausted and so tired of trying—especially when we're attempting to be something, and we're not even sure what it is. Based on narrow-minded and unrealistic images that we've allowed ourselves to be fed from the media, Hollywood, and the fashion industry, most of us have a concept of beauty that takes us to about 25 years of age and then rockets ahead to the elegance and refinement of the 60-year-old woman, with no-man's-land in between. We let advertisers show us how to create the look of ease with expensive-yet-comfortable-looking jeans and the perfect "sloppy" sweater, yet we aren't truly at ease because as long as we're "trying," we still haven't "become." Consequently, our desire is still a craving and not yet an attainment.

Like most women, you might be totally oblivious to the fact that as long as you fearfully "try," you'll never attain—for the mere notion indicates a state of lack (according to the Law of Attraction, you can only bring to yourself what you put out). The saying "fear and it will appear" couldn't be closer to the truth: As long as you're staring into the mirror wishing for something else—dissecting your skin, layering it with anti-aging creams, wishing you looked better, prettier, or younger—you'll never feel a true sense of confidence and contentment. As long as you're exercising with self-punishment, or eating (or not eating) foods with paranoia and worry, you'll only attract back more paranoia, fear, and desire. Moreover, *trying* is such a low-energy word, and it's shrouded in doubt and discouragement: "I doubt I'll lose weight. I doubt my skin will clear up. I doubt he'll think I'm sexy. I doubt I'll find someone to love. I doubt I'll ever be beautiful . . . *but I'll try anyway.*"

The truth is that even with all our newfound feminist strength, and the supposed rejection of the stereotypical beauty standards that we've watched and listened to for far too long, many of us do still believe that our looks are subjective, and that unless we're a size-seven with high cheekbones and flawless skin, we won't be beautiful—and what's worse, we may not find everlasting love without it. We may even ache with an uneasiness when bombarded with young, scantily clad women in magazines, on television, and in movies, while we convince ourselves that it's merely our own lack of confidence and our own flaws and imperfections that make us uncomfortable. Too many of us have inadvertently renounced our own ability to innately trust in and know what *is.*

Nancy Etcoff, the author of the eye-opening book *Survival of the Prettiest: The Science of Beauty,* believes that the reason we're so preoccupied with our looks has to do with one basic factor: sex. She says that our need to procreate is inherently part of us and that our desire for beauty is not a learned condition at all, but rather a biological one. And yet, although I agree that we're absolutely driven at times by our hormones and biology, I must wonder, *Is wanting sex or needing to procreate really what drives us to want to look better?*

In a world where childless (by choice) couples and plastic surgery for postmenopausal women is becoming ever more popular, we must consider the possibility that it could also be our yearning to be accepted, needed, wanted, approved of, and unconditionally loved that has us trying so hard to be someone other than ourselves. Perhaps deep down we fear that if the world knew who we "really" were, it would be disappointed . . . maybe even shocked. So instead, we search for and find masks, facades, and smokescreens to make us "appear" whole, all the while believing that if we could just be "a little better . . . a little prettier . . . a little thinner . . . and look a little younger," we'd have more fun, more luck, and ultimately more love and joy in our lives. Unfortunately, however, until we learn to take our masks off and explore *all* parts of ourselves with love, honor, and acceptance, we'll forever feel insecure, worrying and comparing.

This Book Will Help You Transcend

Over the next couple hundred pages, you'll discover how to love the skin you're in, and then to intuitively attract serenity and passion, eliminate negativity, surround yourself with those who inspire you to be your best, follow the path that's right for your life, and be the most beautiful *you* possible. And this is not about changing who you are, but rather espousing and accessing the unlimited source of beauty and power that's available to us all!

The journey we're about to take requires honesty, integrity, faith, compassion, accountability, and your choice to *let go and become*— that is, to tear down your walls and discover the real you. For once you truly begin to know and like yourself, transcendent beauty will organically follow. One day very soon, you'll find yourself wondering, *Did my exterior change and become breathtakingly beautiful, or did I simply change my perceptions and now I "see beautiful"?* What's even more important is that you won't really care—you'll see and experience beauty in all that you do. And then you'll be free: Free to soar in all your magnificence and be the shining star that you are! As the Persian poet Rumi said, "By God, when you see your beauty, you'll be the idol of yourself."

Before we get started, I suggest that you get yourself a journal, as it will become your greatest guide. You can't achieve a state of transcendence without doing the written work and deepest contemplations. This is not, however, another book that tells you to "try harder"—instead, it's designed to help you excavate the flawless diamond that's buried within you and to show you how to shine it up to a beautiful brilliance! Just as the butterfly emerges from her cocoon, *you* will wake up one day realizing that you're no longer *trying* to be beautiful—you *are!*

Transcendent beauty is my belief for you—a touch of grace for all women, young and old, to see that they, too, can feel irresistible, sexy, healthy, confident, and completely content with their reflection. I pray that you'll embrace it with the same love and passion it was written with!

Shine!

Chapter One

Beauty Is in the Soul

To understand how transcendent beauty is created and accessed, it's necessary for you to first understand "what" and "who" you really are . . . which is what this chapter is all about.

Let Your Light Shine

Did you know that although to the naked eye we may appear to be physical bodies composed of solid matter broken down into molecules and atoms, we're in fact organisms of pure energy? It's true! Quantum physics tells us that we're actually composed of subatomic particles of bundles of energy all vibrating at various speeds. And to top it off . . . *the particles are 99.99 percent empty.*

Imagine—in essence, we're almost not even here! This doesn't just apply to us human beings either, but to all matter, from the book you're reading to the chair you're sitting on and the front door that locks strangers out of your home. In fact, Albert Einstein concluded that matter and energy are perfectly interchangeable, so you can think of matter as the heaviest form of energy, and energy as the lightest form of matter.

Have you ever noticed that when we meet people who "light up the room," we often say that they're beautiful? Regardless of their physical features or the outfits they're wearing, we just know that these individuals have something special, a sparkle deep within. We're naturally drawn to them. They shine, and their energy is intoxicating!

So, what exactly do they possess? And how can we acquire it, too?

The Essence of All Life

Don't confuse energy with the liveliness of a 20-year-old aerobics instructor—rather, *everything* is energy, from the sun, stars, and moon to trees, flowers, animals, and plants. Nature gives off an abundance of energy; in fact, the food we eat when digested becomes energy called a "calorie." Lights, music, computers, television, and radio all give off energy, resonating at different speeds. (Just think how great music can lift your spirits or how a disturbing movie can dampen your mood.)

Think of yourself as an "energy-processing system." While this might sound technical, each of us is in fact processing everything—from the air we breathe to the food we eat, the thoughts we think, the sounds we hear, the words we speak, the images we see, and the emotions we feel—which all create energy within our body. According to Dr. David Hawkins, the brilliant author of *Power vs. Force,* by using the science of kinesiology, scientists are able to determine the speed that each level of consciousness vibrates at. That is, when we have thoughts that are happy and positive, our energetic frequency vibrates very quickly, while when we have negative thoughts, our energy essentially downshifts. Emotions of love and joy are light and vibrant, while those of shame and guilt are dark and almost stagnant. When we speak words that are kind and thoughtful, we raise our resonance by leaps and bounds, while hurtful and cruel ones lower our energy to a dark and heavy state. Energetic frequency is never static—we're always in a state of flux, depending upon our mood, our surroundings, the foods we eat, and the thoughts we think. It's important to remember that energy can never be lost, only transferred.

I know that all this may sound confusing, but it's really quite simple. In fact, my eight-year-old daughter, Julia, came up with the perfect analogy when I was explaining how we each have the choice as to how bright our light shines. She ran over to the dimmer switch on the wall of our dining room and asked, "Like this?" As she turned the knob all the way up, the full spectrum of light beamed out across the room, and she said, "This is someone who's nice and loves everyone." And then she slowly lowered it down, pretending that she was frightened. "This is someone who's mean and afraid," she said.

"Yes, you've got it!" I told her, impressed. "We're all born with a 100-watt bulb inside of us, so to speak, that brilliantly shines through every pore in our body. When we love and treat ourselves and all others with respect, dignity, compassion, and kindness, our light radiantly shines for the whole world to see. But when we stop loving, we stop shining—we barely give off any light at all. And remember, we attract people who shine with the same 'wattage' as we do! So, if you want to have great people in your life, be great yourself!"

Those who live with this awe-inspiring resonance on a daily basis have engaged in the deliberate choice of aligning their energy to the highest levels of universal frequency. As Gary Zukav says in his incredible book *The Seat of the Soul,* "When you shift the level of your consciousness, you shift the frequency of your light." In other words, the more consciously aware you are, the brighter you shine and the more radiant you look and feel.

For many years the word *consciousness* was used only in the physical realm, as nothing more than the function of the brain, such as, "He hit his head and lost consciousness." But these

Feel Your Own Energy

Try to feel the electromagnetic energies coming from your body by holding the palms of your hand facing each other about two inches apart. Wait a few seconds, and then you should feel something. (However, if you're nervous or your hands are cold it will hamper the energies.)

Once you start to sense the electromagnetic energies between your palms, move them slowly to and fro. This is your aura! Try moving your palms farther and farther apart gradually . . . see how far you can go before you no longer feel the magnetic draw and push. Be sure to move your hands deliberately and slowly.

Now try pointing your fingers toward each other and feel those energies, and again move your fingertips to and fro. You also can try this with another person—it's really neat!

days we know that it's actually something profoundly deeper: When an idea suddenly makes perfect sense, we say, "It was like a light came on," which perfectly defines the word *enlightened*. Awareness, or consciousness, is like an awakening where you suddenly become acutely aware that you already have all the answers within you (for example, that you were created in the likeness of perfection), so you intuitively embrace your reflection with ease and contentedness. This is when fear and attachment are suddenly rendered obsolete and when everyone, and everything, in the world becomes exquisitely beautiful. It's when time stands still.

However, shifting our internal resonance to the highest levels of consciousness is not a choice made by the mind; instead, these shifts happen on a level driven by the soul. And sustaining the shift is the secret to maintaining the centered, seemingly miraculous, breathtaking beauty that's the theme of this book.

Since everything from the thoughts we think to the words we speak, how we nurture ourselves and each other, the surroundings we live in, whom we associate with, and even the way we handle stress is energy, then *understanding energy is crucial*. Compare it to this Zen parable: A fish prince one day asks his mother, "What is this 'water' that I keep hearing about from everyone? I'm not sure what it is!" To which his mother replies, "You were born in water, and you will die in it. It flows through you and around you. It's so much a part of you that you're unaware of it."

Snakes and Ladders

Achieving transcendent beauty is very much like playing the once-very-popular children's board game *Snakes and Ladders,* which is believed to date back to India in the 2nd century B.C. (These days, Americans know the game better as *Chutes and Ladders.*) Think of the top of the game as achieving pure enlightenment or blissful beauty—this is authentic power, without force or control. Along the way, we land on ladders that catapult us a few levels at a time: We experience joy, clarity, love, and perhaps even intense intuition. We unknowingly emit a beautiful aura that surrounds our physical body. We feel amazing and look extraordinary, and everyone is naturally drawn to us.

On the other hand, we also land on snake tails that pull us back down, leaving us feeling unattractive, insecure, depressed, and even lost. Our energetic frequency dramatically drops, our aura becomes dull and dark, and we feel powerless and alone.

To help you better understand how energy affects your beauty, think about how you feel after you've gossiped or betrayed someone, or even just after you've sat in front of a computer monitor for far too long: You most likely felt drained and low. Conversely, remember the electricity you felt when falling in love or the rush of vitality you experienced after achieving a great accomplishment—you were alive and glowing!

Everyone in the world is playing this game of *Snakes and Ladders,* yet most are unconscious of it. Nevertheless, any person, at any given time, can be calibrated to determine the level of energy they're vibrating at. When we come from a position of love and fearlessness, our energy is intensely powerful—so much so, in fact, that we may not even recognize how much we've transcended. That's because we're no longer aware of it, nor do we even worry or think about it. As our beauty moves into this innate sense of knowingness, it actually becomes inconsequential to us because we no longer carry the low-vibrating energy of lack or approval. We feel calm, content, and serene, even though to the outside world we're overwhelmingly powerful.

On the other hand, when we come from a position of fear, our energy is very weak and heavy, and the only way we can execute it is by force. We must push our way on to people and manipulate things to go our way. We demand answers when we want them, and we insist that people treat us in the way we think we deserve to be treated or we discard them. We expect things to go our way, and we feel hurt or disappointed when they don't.

Jesus Christ and Buddha lived with the highest levels of human consciousness, transcending beauty into an effortless and enlightened state. This is the quest for all of us, for the more energy we have, the more powerful we are. As we begin to abide by the powerfully potent energies of trust, faith, love, and detachment, our world becomes exactly as it should, and we understand the saying "When everything is meant to be, it just falls perfectly into place!"

Absolute Energy Equals Absolute Beauty

So, in our quest for transcendent beauty we must become acutely aware of our level of consciousness. We must attract positive energies and resist downshifting to the negative. In other words, absolute energy equals absolute power, which equates to absolute beauty. Unfortunately, for many women this concept is an oxymoron. They wonder, *How can beauty and power be one in the same?* It seems that even with all the gains we've made in the last hundred years, too many of us are still afraid to be truly powerful . . . to be completely magnificent . . . to be transcendentally beautiful!

We unconsciously give our power away all the time to everyone in our lives—and losing massive amounts in the process to our own feelings of guilt, shame, regret, or even pride. Some of us lose our power while procrastinating or blaming others, while some squander it away on jealousy or envy . . . yet most of us unconsciously give our power away to fear. We've been taught to associate power with negative connotations—words such as *control, aggression, manipulation,* and even *bitchiness.*

Many of us are afraid that we'll be judged if we become truly powerful; that others won't approve of us if we start climbing ladders and will ask, "Who does she think she is?" Maybe we're afraid that we might look conceited, or even worse, that we might be unlovable if we have it together too much. Perhaps we give our power away because we actually fear ourselves . . . our own strength. As Marianne Williamson says in *A Return to Love:* "It is our light, not our darkness, that most frightens us. We ask ourselves, 'Who am I to be brilliant, gorgeous, talented, fabulous?' Actually who are you *not* to be? You are a child of God. Your playing small doesn't serve the world. There's nothing enlightened about shrinking so that other people won't feel insecure around you. . . . We were born to manifest the glory of God that is within us."

Are you ready to be your most beautiful and powerful self? Are you ready to become the woman you were always meant to be—to claim your power and to access that magnificent light waiting to shine from deep inside of you?

Well, in order to do that, you must understand how we women have gotten here and what we've come through. . . .

The Last 40 Years

When feminism came along, it empowered women to fight for their rights and stand up for themselves, screaming out that self-love was what mattered most, that the "love" too many females were living with was without essence and was, in fact, really only oppression. The patriarchal world that had, up until then, dictated their every choice was suddenly denounced as many women ditched their bras, rejected sexual comments, and viewed lipstick and lingerie as frivolous and exploitive. (Many also saw those who dyed their hair blonder or wore their bras tighter as the adversaries.) Demanding that their own identities finally be heard, many feminists were angry and tired of being demoralized—they knew what their foremothers had gone through, and most simply wanted to change the world for women to come. While many were angry men haters, not all were, yet the world ended up labeling all feminists as angry lesbians. The result was that lots of strong and determined women were left completely confused about their own beauty, love, and life itself. Nevertheless, they fought on. . . .

At the same time, another group of females began to emerge—those who depended all the more upon their looks and sexuality to achieve status and success. While peering over at the strong and mighty advances of feminists, their own anger brewed. Many felt ashamed of the way they'd allowed men to manipulate them, yet they depended upon the attention and fringe benefits that it brought. Deep down most secretly worried about their own futures, when their looks would dwindle and their breasts would sag: Would they still be beautiful? Would they still be taken care of? Would they still be loved? Too fearful to look back and yet even more afraid to look forward, many got caught in the trap of disillusionment as they *also* felt panicked about their beauty, love, and life itself.

A civil war was looming, and the lines were drawn: Those who rejected beauty as their means to advance were opposed to those who used it, with the rest of women caught somewhere in the middle. The terrified ladies left on the sidelines were so shocked and nervous over what was happening that they clung to their aprons all the more, figuring that if they just buried their heads in the sand, cooked another meal, darned another sock, and pretended that everything was just fine, then everything would be. These unfortunates were so self-deprived that most of their needs, whether sexual, emotional, or intellectual, were often overlooked. These were women who had lost their passion and felt totally powerless. And many of them were our own mothers and grandmothers.

Nothing like this battle had ever happened on such a grand scale to women before. They weren't just at war with men anymore, they were now engaged in combat with each other, not realizing that they were all desperate for the same things—respect, love, appreciation, and contentment; to just *be* and to know that they alone were enough.

Throughout the '80s and '90s the battle intensified, and soon women were demanding and expecting the same equalities as men, without realizing that they were no longer gaining ground. Many females in the corporate world were turning into little replicas of men, believing that if they talked louder, walked faster, glared harder, and showed less compassion and more force they'd finally get the respect they deserved. Unfortunately, they didn't recognize that true power could never be demanded or enforced; rather, it can only come from embracing femininity, sexuality, and intelligence with passion, acceptance, understanding, strength, grace, gentleness, and kindness. It then transcends when all women welcome each other with the same honor and dignity.

Instead, many of us were convinced that once men were made accountable for their "wrongdoings" that our lives would work out and we'd find serenity, peace, and soon—*very soon*—we'd feel beautiful. But that didn't seem to come about . . . in fact, we appeared to be even less happy about our looks, bodies, and sexuality. What was happening?

Well, we watched our mothers fight the fight (or depending on your age, you fought it yourself), yet we intrinsically felt their deep yearning to still nurture and love. They were so confused—trying to be feminists and rejecting the beauty myth, while still instinctively knowing that love and companionship were what mattered most. It was no one's fault, but the messages got mixed and the beliefs that most passed down to us, their daughters, were shaky. We were told that men exploited us and that beauty wasn't important, as we watched our moms continue to read beauty magazines, pack themselves into their girdles, and coat their skin with the latest wrinkle cream. They swallowed the "pill," so to speak, and then got mad that it was provided. We, then, quite literally swallowed a few more, often by the name of Prozac, Paxil, Zoloft, or Effexor (the total sales worldwide of antidepressants in 2002 was nearly 27 million prescriptions), in an attempt to numb our scattered emotions and frustrations, all the while angrily comparing ourselves to the 17-year-old model on the cover of the magazine that *we'd* just bought.

And, yes, although we're much further ahead now than ever before, too many of us are still in a frustrated, even frantic, state, listening to the unrelenting disparagement of our chattering minds, telling us what we should have done and still need to do, while pointing out the more perfect outfit, the more perfect home, the more perfect marriage, and the more perfect woman.

Like it or not, we women have allowed ourselves to play a game we can never win. It's based on conforming and changing, competing and comparing, starving and denying, and hurting and hoarding. Sadly, it seems that we know more about what celebrities are wearing and who they're romancing than we do about our own needs and desires, and we're more aware of the latest fashion trends than our own purpose and passion. It's too bad that we've allowed ourselves to buy into it, but I do believe that this *is* changing.

Slowly but surely, we're realizing that our magnificent beauty and strength will only transcend when we join together as sisters—as mirror reflections of our own beautiful souls. We must breathe each other in, celebrate our splendor, and rejoice in our power, knowing that we are exactly as we should be. We must create a world in which stock-market portfolios and perfume can go hand in hand; where we happily regard men as our much-needed partners and no longer our oppressors; where beauty can be celebrated with wild, long black hair or seized in a short blonde crop; where breast size has nothing to do with intelligence or sincerity; and where we lovingly respect and honor our femininity, without pressure or expectation.

It's time that we stop living with this fear-driven force and begin accessing the unstoppable and limitless source of authentic power that's deep within each of us. Lipstick and lingerie are not the enemy, yet neither is detachment and autonomy. The time has come for us to enter into a new era where we claim who we are! We must embrace our differences and accept and revere what makes us so uniquely female. No longer should we gauge our success and beauty using each other as our barometers, or compete to get the "best man" who will give us the best life.

It's ultimately time to appreciate ourselves and each other—consciously excited that beauty is diverse and nothing, not even time, can steal it away. As I tell my daughters every day, "Love your body, and it will love you back!"

Without Apologies

As David Hawkins explains in his book, power is very different from force. Force is a frenetic, chaotic-type of faltering energy that comes with highs and lows, while power is a magnificent confidence that can never be taken from you nor enforced on anyone else. Power is peaceful. Power is potent. Power is perfection. And power transcends beauty.

Think of some of the most genuinely beautiful women who have lived or are still living: Oprah Winfrey, Sophia Loren, Julia Roberts, Tina Turner, Audrey Hepburn, Susan Sarandon, Maya Angelou, Mother Teresa, Jackie Kennedy, and Princess Diana, plus the millions of unknowns who have surrendered to their love and passion at the deepest core. Women who accept themselves for who they are, without apologies, and who magically exude a gentle strength and humble confidence through every pore in their bodies. These beauties have aligned their energy with that of their love and purpose, not their fears and worries. They're authentically powerful, and they've owned it. I'm sure that these incredible women also know that it's not just the thoughts they think, the food they eat, or the words they speak that will raise or lower their energy, but rather the attachment they've placed on the truth of their perceptions.

In other words, as long as you hold on to your idea of what's beautiful, then no matter how many times you tell yourself to think beautiful thoughts, you'll still be attached to a preconceived notion of beauty. And unless you can align your energy with your concept, then achieving it is impossible . . . at least in your mind. And since your brain cannot separate perception from reality (and is there really only one reality?), it will always align your energy with your awareness of the truth. If your truth is that beauty is only found in long legs, blonde hair, blue eyes, and a size-C bra,

It seems that beauty's elusiveness is a worldwide phenomenon. According to "The Real Truth about Beauty: A Global Report," of the 3,200 women surveyed in a Dove-commissioned study that spanned the globe, only 2 percent of women considered themselves "beautiful," and even less than that of the women surveyed in Canada—only 1 percent thought they were. Do we really live in a world where less than 2 percent of the women are beautiful?

but you're petite with black hair, brown eyes, and an A cup, how will your energy ever align with that of acceptance, abundance, love, and bliss? How will you ever transcend beauty? Well, you'll probably just end up trying harder.

But what if you could change your definition of what beautiful, ideal, and perfect are at the cellular level? What if you could realign your energy with a new belief that could transform your perception of reality, reexamine your concept of beauty, and amend your interpretation of your experiences to make them positive and to elevate your brilliance from deep within? What if you could redefine your notion of what's beautiful so that you'll *always* fit it?

Well, you can!

But first, let's go back to when your energy was brightest and your beauty transcended.

Your Earliest Beginnings

At the moment of conception, your soul filled you with a radiant light, as it gently whispered that you're beautiful. Then you grew inside your mother's womb, feeling her emotional state and aligning with her energetic frequency: If she was overjoyed to be pregnant, then every single one of your cells knew that they were loved and resonated with bliss. If the pregnancy was unwanted, however, her sadness flowed through and around you, and your cells heaved with heaviness. Yet, regardless of whether your conception was deemed a "mistake" or was 100 percent planned, your soul knew exactly why it chose your parents, realizing that the very miracle of life could conquer all.

When you were born, your mother (whether biological or adopted) picked you up and held you in her arms—filled with so much love as your energy flowed through and around her, she felt more alive as her beauty was transcended. For that brief moment you were a precise mirror reflection of each other and your energies were perfectly aligned. Your great-great-great-great-great-great grandmother sang, and all your ancestors rejoiced. You had arrived! Your soul was revealed, and you were shining in your perfect glory.

As you grew into a toddler, you danced and played, celebrating your beauty with effortlessness and comfort. Without doubt or conceit, you knew with absolute certainty that you were beautiful. Why wouldn't everyone adore you?

By the time you were three or four, you looked to your mother with reverence: All knowing and so wise, you watched the way she embraced herself and the world. You saw the way your dad treated her, and you believed everything she said to be the truth—her ideas, attitudes, and actions were deeply ingrained into you. You listened to the way she spoke about herself and about you, and you took it all in and decided what life for a woman would be like.

Over the next seven or eight years, you began to become aware of the world around you, unconsciously making observations about what was beautiful, who was popular, and how you fit into the hierarchy. Watching your parents, caretakers, teachers, and siblings—while listening to what they said to and about you—a new clandestine voice in your mind emerged and began to draw conclusions about your looks, intelligence, personality, even how lovable you were. It started whispering into your ear, telling you what you should have done, how you should have acted, or what you should have looked like.

This "mind-made self" is also known as the ego, and it's always trying . . . always thinking . . . always wanting to be in control. Each time you listen to it, your light dims!

The Mind-Made Self

Shaped primarily in your formative years, your mind-made self or ego can be found simply by listening to the chatter that incessantly carries on in your brain: the repetitive messages that replay over and over that you assume you have no control of, which developed just around the time you began to believe that you were separate and detached from your parents.

If you came from fearless folks who were filled with trust, passion, purpose, and kindness; and who trusted in the world and who knew that love would conquer all, then there's a good chance that you, too, shine with this same fearless power. But if you suffered from abuse, neglect, or just a fear-driven upbringing, you probably developed a loud and destructive ego. Sewn together on all the worries and fears of the women before you, as well as the messages you grew up hearing, this voice is simply an illusion of you, and if you listen to it long enough, you'll become so distracted from the real you—your higher self—that your light, once vibrant and radiant, will become dull and dim.

Can you hear your ego talking to you? What does it whisper into your ears? What does it say when you look into the mirror? Does it mutter that your skin isn't youthful enough or that your nose is too big? Maybe it lets you know that you aren't tall or thin enough, as it simultaneously recognizes the "perfect" height or weight of someone else. It can be the voice that reminds you that no one can be trusted and that you can really only count on you, and that love is a lie and that you'll end up getting hurt. Maybe it tells you that you're inadequate and that you'll never succeed, or that you're a flake, disorganized, or unworthy. For most of us, though, the voice tells us that we'll never be beautiful.

Now, stop reading for a minute and notice that your mind-made self has been silent as you've read. As you sit in this moment of calm, recognize this "I of the mind"—this illusion of yourself—from the "real you." Can you differentiate the voice of your ego?

Can you think of some of the things it says to you when you're feeling down, discouraged, or afraid? What are some of the nasty belittling remarks it feeds you?

Your ego is the heaviest, or slowest-vibrating, energy within you, and if you abide by it you'll become heavy, depressed, dark, and ugly yourself. If you listen to it, you'll unconsciously sabotage yourself because every choice you make will support the learned beliefs that it deems to be true.

Learned beliefs are different from logical beliefs. They're the deepest internal opinions we carry about ourselves and the world around us, and they direct our lives. Logical beliefs are the profound politically correct views we share with the world, but they're not the beliefs that drive us. For example, a logical belief is one such as: "I know that beauty is diverse and can be found in all women." Yet a learned belief might reveal something far different: "I don't think I'm beautiful."

When it comes to your own beauty (or any situation in your life), ask yourself the following questions, writing down your answers in your journal:

- What are my learned beliefs about myself, my looks and body, and my ability to love and receive love? What have I learned about succeeding and how to maintain that success?

- Where did I learn these beliefs? Who told them to me?

- Are these beliefs serving me now? If not, what am I losing by believing them? How are they holding me back in life? What are they costing me? And just as important, what am I gaining by believing them? How are they working for me? And how have they become my excuse for my not becoming the woman I'm meant to be?

These questions will open up the door for you to begin understanding who you are, what you believe about yourself, and how you've allowed your ego to direct your life. It's not surprising to discover that you'll always make choices to support your learned beliefs . . . *always!* You can't consciously choose otherwise because you're set up to trust in your thoughts and abide by your "inner voice." Even when success begins to happen, if it doesn't line up with your learned beliefs, you'll unconsciously self-sabotage, and you won't figure out why you keep doing it!

Basically, it works like this: If your belief is that men can't be trusted, not only will you subconsciously seek out untrustworthy men, you'll also create drama and scenarios to constantly test their trustworthiness. You'll actually set them up to betray you . . . and then wait for it to happen! Finally, if some special man *does* jump over all your hurdles, you'll regain a touch of trust, but throughout the entire relationship, you'll end up testing and taunting him, waiting for him to fail. Security will never be yours—you set it up that way based on your beliefs.

Let's say you believe that you're unattractive and unlikely to ever be beautiful and sexy—well, no matter what diet you start, what skin creams you apply, or what plastic surgery you have, you're going to fall off track, give up, and still find more wrinkles and other things you think you need to fix.

The bottom line is if your mind believes that you're destined to fail—or that people are destined to fail you—it's going to create circumstances and situations to work against you. Your ego would rather be right than have peace; after all, winning is always what matters most! Therefore, based on your beliefs, as a small child you began to "co-create" your life. You made choices, each and every day, based on these beliefs and developed ways of reacting and responding. And now you're a culmination of each one of those choices. So ask yourself: *Am I happy with my life? Am I happy with myself? Am I happy with my choices?*

To begin to attract beauty, love, success, and peace into your life, you must realize that you've set your life up to get what you believe you deserve from it. You've decided whether or not to listen to your ego—you're not an innocent bystander in your own life.

The Higher Self

Many people confuse the *higher self* with something religious, but it is, in fact, who you are. It's the central force with which you were intended to live, love, think, and dwell—it's perfect, fearless, trusting, pure, and passionate, and it knows with absolute certainty that you're exquisitely perfect, too. Your higher self is your soul, the lightest, or fastest-vibrating, form of energy within your body. When it's revealed, your beauty is transcended. When you enter a room, people literally stop and stare because they can feel it. It's impossible not to!

Your higher self is always at ease, trusting in and appreciating the beauty you already possess. It sees the beauty in all things, and in all people, at all times. When you abide by your higher self, rather than your ego, your life feels meaningful, your energy is powerful, and your beauty is transcended into exquisiteness.

Your higher self is an infinite part of a "Higher Power" that is the essence of all life. Mysterious, mystical, and omnipotent, some call their Higher Power "The Divine," while others call it "The Universe," and many prefer to think of it simply as "The Light." Although I think of my Higher Power as "God," I often refer to it as the "Divine Universal Collective Energy."

The most important aspect is not to get caught up in the word used to describe it, for words don't matter—they're subjective and unimportant. It's our earthly tribalism that causes us to argue about this never-ending, never-diminishing "ocean" of love and radiant light. Just know that it's completely universal and makes no exception for race or religion. God needs no name—(S)he knows What (S)he is. It's our need for attachment—our desire to be acknowledged—that makes us assume (S)he does, too.

Your soul is like a gallon of water scooped from this sea of all-knowing wisdom, and although your soul is no longer in the body of water, it will always be part of it. Your soul is the God within you and is immortal. You—the person walking, talking, and bearing your name—is merely the container it resides in. God created us to experience life in a way He couldn't as only a spiritual being. He divided us up into millions of tiny parts—souls—and sent us down here to learn and discover . . . to evolve. Never forget that we're all connected. We're all soul sisters, we're all Divine, and we're all absolutely beautiful! The ancient Indian sages professed that "fear is born of separation." When you choose to see yourself as separate and isolated, whether it's from a friend, your family, a stranger, or even from nature and animals, you evoke fear and chaos from within. And this fear is the breeding ground of the ego.

The Intellectual Self

The mind is not the enemy. It was created for a specific purpose: to process and translate our experiences in the physical world to our higher self. When we feel safe, confident, and secure, we man-age our emotions via our "intellectual self," using wisdom and compassion, and then we organically transmit our experiences on to our higher self. Our higher self learns a new lesson—climbs a ladder, as it were—and every one of our cells rejoices with this transcendence.

Again, stop reading for a moment and close your eyes. Can you visualize your soul? Can you feel something deep within you? A beautiful light? Perhaps just the presence of something powerful? Is it in your chest? In your abdominal area? Your heart? Your mind? Where is it? Feel the God within you.

Do you feel stronger as you become aware of this inner light? (Don't worry if this is hard for you to do, especially if you feel as if you've been disconnected from your higher self. Simply meditate each morning for five minutes on "seeing" your higher self in your mind's eye, and soon you'll begin to feel the soul within you.)

Now, can you picture your soul? What does she look like? Is she you as your most beautiful self? Is she angelic looking? Is she tall or tiny? Does she have long flowing hair or is it short? What is she wearing? Is she smiling? Is she serious? What does she say to you? What beliefs does she hold for your life? If you were to read her the learned beliefs you wrote out in the journal, what do you think she'd say about them?

Finally, ask yourself which voice you'd rather listen to: your ego or your soul?

Each experience we go through was designed to discover and heal aspects of our consciousness, in order for our soul to evolve. Our higher self can only do this by experiencing the physical world—there's no other reason for us to be here. Once our higher self receives the messages from the intellectual self, it gently answers us back and guides us with perfect ease, in every situation.

Ourintellectualselfconnects our body to our soul the way our spinal cord connects our body to our brain, and our intuition is the voice of our soul talking back. When we abide by our soul, we're destined for greatness because we intrinsically know that everything is as it should be. We're relaxed, calm, and content, and we exude a gentle yet magnificent energy. This is the body-mind-soul connection.

21 Grams of Pure Power

When I found out that upon our last breath, every human being loses 21 grams of body weight, I was in awe. *Everyone*—from a tiny baby to a monster of a man—loses 21 grams at death. The size of a hummingbird, those 21 grams of pure power comprise your precious soul.

To understand authentic power you must understand that your soul is immortal. It existed before you were born and it will exist after you die. It chooses a "body" and a "personality" in order to learn the lessons it needs to learn, but once you die, your soul continues to live on. It returns home to the universal collective of love and light . . . back to the "universal ocean" . . . back to Heaven. As Gary Zukav says in *The Mind of the Soul:* "Your lifetime is one chapter in a book, and the book is your soul."

The Battle Within

As you can see, the mind can be your best friend or your greatest foe, depending on which "self" you choose to direct your thinking. Your mind-made and higher selves have very different intentions that, depending on which one you abide by, will set your life in one direction or the other. The mind-made self is the cause of all your cravings, frustrations, wants, and desires, as it is in a constant pursuit of "things," without realizing that its hunger can never be satisfied. It creates judgments and attaches to outcome—it loves when you label yourself with disorders, dysfunction, and addictions, or with words such as *dumb, jealous,* or *ugly.* That way it can always be trying to fix you—reiterating over and over to your subconscious that you're flawed and powerless.

Your ego is the part of you that gets offended and hurt. It's opinionated and overly sensitive, competes and compares, has already decided (in its mind) what the nicest color of hair and eyes are, and it believes that it knows whether being tall or short is best. It continues to notice those who have achieved more than you or have better things than you, whether it's a fancier car, a nicer house, a better job, or a sexier body. It's the voice inside your head that convinces you that your dreams are wishful thinking, as it tries to fool you that somewhere "out there" your beauty will be found—that with enough work, usually precipitated by self-loathing and punishment, you may eventually attain it. But you never do—and never can—because the ego is never satisfied.

In spite of this, the ego is within us and is a part of us—one that we'll never be able to completely eradicate—so by fighting it, we make it our enemy. Our ego is the most basic, animalistic side of our consciousness. When it senses what it believes is too much danger, it tries to take over and comes out swinging. The trouble is that it fights against us without even realizing the damage it's doing. It truly doesn't know that our intellectual self is connected to our higher self and that when we abide by our soul, success without fear, obsession, or anxiety organically grows, and we live in harmony—our health is abundant, our bodies are agile and fit, our skin and hair glow, and our mind is vibrant and inspired.

But since our soul will never fight (as it has no personal will), annihilating the ego would serve no purpose, even if it could be accomplished. The soul knows that suppression, oppression, and repression are never constructive ways to deal with anything. Besides, we can all agree that "whatever we resist, persists." To end the battle and to live with transcendent beauty, we must learn how to tame the beast and make it our ally.

Soulful Beauty

While most people talk about beauty as merely physical, the truth is that nothing has more soul. Yet, sadly, so many allow this dark saboteur, in its fearful need for control, to shadow their light, as it instructs them to try harder, to look further, and to expect something more—and if left unchecked, it will talk so much that they can barely hear anything else.

How many of us are trying to sort through our painful experiences, hurtful words, and disappointments—sometimes even including extreme cases of betrayal, neglect, and abuse (be it verbal, physical, or sexual)—on our own? We don't realize that we're directly connected to the Divine Universal Collective Energy of omnipotent power and beauty, which has all the answers if we'd only listen.

The truth is that too many of us have lost faith in our higher self. Often feeling so alone, insecure, and unsure, we occasionally cry out to a God somewhere "out there," not realizing that our soul is the God within, gently and consistently waiting to guide, love, nurture, and reassure us. Our soul will never forsake or wrongly lead us . . . *ever!*

So many of us ache to achieve a feeling of contentment, courage, and confidence—one that we may have only experienced under the influence of drugs or alcohol, or while shopping or seducing. And most of us are totally unaware that strength and power only come through an inner transcendence of ego, where we become one with Divine grace, where we innately know that God is within and part of all of us, and where we *are* love and love *is* us.

It's heartbreaking that so many of us would rather believe that we're in control and that if we get focused and tough enough and make the right choices, our lives will work out and we'll eventually find love, serenity, and peace—and we'll feel beautiful—but it never happens and never will as long as our searching, worrying, stressing, and planning continues. Remember that the ego *tries* but can never *be,* while the soul simply *is. . . .*

The Body-Mind-Soul Connection

Most of us are quite confused about the definition of the *ego.* We often associate it with the loud, boastful guy who always has to be right, but it's merely that nonstop voice inside our heads that tells us who it thinks we are and who it thinks we should be based on what we saw, heard, and felt while growing up. Think of it as our fears amplified.

However, it's based only on our *perception* of reality, which is why some of the most beautiful women see themselves as ugly, the most intelligent feel stupid, and some of the kindest think that they're boring. Looking into the mirror through the shadowed eyes of the ego, rather than that of their soul, these women only see what their mind-made self tells them to see, and over time its messages begin to permeate into every cell in their body. Soon, their skin feels ugly, their nails begin to think that they're unsightly, and even their organs and immune system begin to lose their splendor, as this "I" of the mind can actually begin to change the body's biology.

The mind is ultimately responsible for all of our illnesses, from things such as migraine headaches to cancer, chronic fatigue to depression, and anorexia to obesity. The body is merely the messenger, and the ego, if given the opportunity, will chitchat with every single one of our 100 trillion cells, convincing them of whatever negativity it is focused on. The energy levels in the cells thus become slower, heavier, and extremely susceptible to illness. They feel ugly, depressed, and tired . . . and they begin to slow down.

The important thing to realize about illness and disease is that they're actually healing opportunities to figure out what's really going on in your life. I've come to learn that all symptoms manifest in the mind before they ever develop within the body. What's so amazing, though, is that we also have all that we need to heal any illness. *Yes! You heal your body . . . with the power of your mind.*

Although I'm certainly not suggesting that we cause our illnesses consciously, I do believe that we're responsible for them and must become cognizant of our energetic frequency in order to heal them. If we let our ego direct us, we resonate in fear—

right down to the cellular level. But if we choose to let our soul guide us, our cells resonate in love, wellness, joy, and vitality. As Dr. Christiane Northrup, the author of *Women's Bodies, Women's Wisdom,* explains:

> In several scientific studies, inescapable stress has been associated with a distinct form of immunosupression (suppression of immune system response). Emotional shock is associated with the release of endogenous opiates (morphinelike substances) and corticosteroids (hormones form the adrenal glands), which prevent white blood cells from protecting the body from cancer and infection. People who have a sense of hopelessness or despair and who perceive their situation as being uncontrollably stressful have higher levels of corticosteroids and immune suppression than do those who attempt to cope with stress. People who are exposed to what they perceive as inescapable stress actually release opioidlike substances (enkephalins) that literally numb the cells of their bodies (in stress-induced analgesia), rendering them incapable of destroying the cancer cells and bacteria if this goes on chronically. It is not *stress itself* that creates immune system problems. It is, rather, the *perception* that the stress is inescapable—that there is nothing a person can do to prevent it—that is associated with immune suppression. [And] 80 percent of autoimmune diseases affect women rather than men.

In other words, you are what you believe you are, right down to the cellular level. If you change your beliefs, you can change your life!

This reminds me of a situation I had with one of my clients, Jo-Anne Wade. She wrote to tell me that she'd been doing my total transformation program, *Simply . . . Woman!* for six months, and had lost some weight and gone from barely walking a mile to running five. However, she was now back at square one, after suddenly developing the Norwalk virus.

It began with canker sores on her tongue, which developed into tumors that had to be surgically removed. After not being able to swallow properly for months, Jo-Anne had given up exercise, lost all her recently developed muscle, and developed a serious lung infection. She reached out to me, desperately asking, "How could this happen to me after I'd been doing so well?"

The first thing I explained to her was that the body, mind, and soul are connected, and when we get sick, it's not the virus that makes us ill but rather our body's inability to fight it. Each of us has a "weak link" or a spot on the body that's the first to "go" when we're run-down. These weak links are related to different energy systems in the body called *chakras.* Chakras are very real but invisible sensors that process energy entering our body.

For example, our fifth chakra governs our ability to speak our truth and honor our personal will and integrity. Consequently, when we feel as if we can't say what we really mean, or we aren't living the life we know that we're meant to live, we often find ourselves with trouble around the ears, throat, and mouth, including headaches, sore throats, canker and cold sores, and even cervical-spine dysfunction. (For more on chakras, please see Chapter 7.)

I then told Jo-Anne that consistent with Louise Hay's amazing book *You Can Heal Your Life,* the tongue represents "the ability to taste the pleasures of life with joy." Canker sores are "festering words held back by the lips," and tumors symbolize "nursing old hurts and shocks." Lung problems correspond to "our inability to take in life, which is often followed by depression, grief, and not feeling worthy of living life fully."

I asked her to think about how her success with *Simply . . . Woman!* had played out in her life: Did she feel worthy of this new wonderful body? Was she afraid to embrace the "new woman" that she'd become or were there more dreams that she wanted to accomplish that perhaps she was holding herself back from? Was she holding on to past pain? Did she feel as if she could really stand up for herself with personal integrity? Was she speaking her truth? Was she living true to her path and not necessarily the one that seemed perfect to everyone else? Did she honestly believe that she could maintain her success?

I then asked my client to repeat this new thought pattern from *You Can Heal Your Life* every day for 21 days: *"I rejoice in all of my life's bountiful givingness. . . . I lovingly release the past and turn my attention to this new day. . . . I create only joyful experiences in my loving world. . . . All is well."*

Jo-Anne wrote back to tell me that she'd come to the right place in seeking my help. She confided that she and her husband of more than 20 years had broken up awhile back, and she was still nursing some old wounds and sadness. Although she knew that the divorce was absolutely necessary (especially since her husband had been very distant and totally cold during their entire marriage, and she wasn't getting what she needed from the relationship), she still had a hard time letting go. Always wondering "why" and "what could have been," Jo-Anne felt as if she'd never said all she needed to say to her husband—or perhaps it was that she'd never gotten the answers she needed from him in return. The result was that even years later, she still felt "stuck" so much of the time.

A few months later, she posted this testimonial on the message forum at **www.crystalandrus.com**:

> One year ago I purchased *Simply . . . Woman!* and my world has changed in so many incredible ways. But it begins by going back to June 10, 1993, over 12 years ago.
>
> I was working as a municipal law enforcement officer when I got a call to come back to the police station. Once there I was taken into a private office by my sergeant and told that my father had just passed away. Shocked and not knowing how to feel, my mind started thinking about all that my dad had taught me and what he'd meant to me. He always said that it was up to me to get what I wanted out of life, that I needed to surround myself with positive people and not to live with "ifs." He'd say, "Stop saying 'if' and 'when' and just do it!"
>
> As I walked out of the station that day, I saw a very sweaty group of police officers and disabled athletes running in a marathon called the "Law Enforcement Torch Run" that raised money for the physically challenged. At the time it didn't faze me—in fact, it was just a deterrent for me, delaying me from getting to my car to go home and cry. But every single year after that when I'd see the runners go by, the first thing I'd think of was my father and the day I learned that he was gone.

For the last couple of years I wished that I could take part in the run, as it seemed to sum up everything my father had taught me. Seeing these dedicated police officers and disabled children giving it their all motivated me, but I knew that I couldn't run to the end of my driveway, let alone 15 to 20 kilometers in one shot.

Then last year was it—I'd had enough with wishing, and it was time to start doing! After all, I wasn't doing anything for my father's legacy by sitting on my butt!

The day after watching the "Torch Run" for the 12th year I purchased *Simply . . . Woman!* That was on June 4, 2004, exactly one year ago.

Today, I am happy to announce that this year on Monday, June 6, 2005, *I, Jo-Anne Wade, ran the Law Enforcement Torch Run for the Special Olympics!* I did it, and it was amazing! Everything about it, even the temperature of 31 degrees Celsius [88 degrees Fahrenheit] under the blazing sun didn't deter me! I'd reached my goal, and I know that my dad was there egging me on and supporting me the whole way.

I love you, Dad, and I thank you again, Crystal.

Sincerely,

Jo-Anne Wade

I'm happy to tell you that Jo-Anne is now celebrating her second wedding anniversary with the new love of her life. She's finally letting go of the "what-ifs" and "could have beens" and is now beaming with beauty!

Your mind is in every cell of your body.
Your energy shifts on a cellular level to align with the beliefs it carries.
You become what you believe!

Talk to the mirror on the wall
She says I'm not the fairest one
O no not at all
So familiar down so low
And don't matter where I've been
There's nowhere to go
Tired of waiting for my moment to arrive
Tired of painting up my life to survive
Still I found beauty in hard places
When I thought I couldn't make it
and that's where I found you so face it
We found beauty . . . in hard places . . .

— Colette Baron-Reid
Lyrics from her CD *I Am / Grace*

Chapter Two

Lights, Camera, Action!

I remember watching my mother get ready to go out with my father on the occasional Friday evening when I was a young girl. It was the '70s, and she was the flawless combination of Farrah Fawcett and Goldie Hawn: Feathered blonde hair, a perfect white smile, luscious red lips, tanned skin, and huge green eyes painted up like a cat's, she mesmerized everyone, man or woman, who met her gaze. She was the most beautiful woman I'd ever seen, and she and my dad were the perfect couple.

When I studied my own reflection in the mirror, I couldn't help but compare—and all I'd see were lips too big for my tiny face, pale white skin, and boring straight hair that hung past my skinny butt. My older brother reminded me daily of how ugly I was, teasing me beyond anything I can describe. I longed to be a woman . . . I longed to be beautiful . . . I longed to look like my mom.

My mother, on the other hand, loved Scarlett O'Hara, the heroine of *Gone with the Wind,* and by the time I was seven or eight years old, I'd already seen the movie a half dozen times or so. I knew quite matter-of-factly that Scarlett had an 18-inch waist—an hourglass body of perfection. And by age ten, I, not surprisingly, also knew that Marilyn Monroe had measurements of 36-24-36 (or so my mother thought). I'd watch Mom with her measuring tape, comparing. The smaller she could get her waist, the happier she seemed, for she ached to be "tiny." I think she was always on a diet.

Ironically, when my parents split up (I was 12), my mother became a bodybuilder and soon transformed her 115-pound body into a statue of sculpted muscle and power—yet her waist always remained 24 inches. So, by the time I was 15, I was anxiously measuring my own waist, crying when I couldn't get it smaller than 25. It didn't matter that I had legs 3 inches longer than my mom's and hipbones that measured 37 inches wide, without an ounce of fat on them . . . I didn't have a 24-inch waist. I'd never be sexy, with a perfect body. I'd never be the ideal woman.

When I began my own transformative body/mind/soul journey in my late 20s, I realized that for most of my life, I'd been measuring my beauty against other women—actresses, models, and mostly my mother—using them as the barometer of my success. No matter how good I was, I was never good *enough*. And, finally, when perfectionism, eating disorders, and huge weight gains followed by bouts of depression took their toll, I realized that enough was enough—I'd better start doing work on my insides, since all the time I'd spent on the outside never seemed to fix my insecurities. I never saw "beautiful" when I looked in the mirror, which is crazy because when I look back at old pictures, I see now that I *was* a beautiful little girl. It's sad that I truly never saw it at the time.

The River Runs Deep

I've worked with hundreds of women who struggle desperately with their body image, self-esteem, and ability to nurture and honor themselves. When they look in the mirror, they see "ugly," "weak," "unattractive," and most often "overweight" staring back, and they speak about themselves worse than any enemy ever could. These individuals view the world as a scary place, filled with dishonest people who could hurt them—and they don't even realize that they're re-creating the same emotional atmosphere, or energetic resonance, that they grew up in.

Keep in mind that the word *familiar* comes from *family*. That is, we do what we know . . . which is what's most comfortable to us. Therefore, our job as self-empowered adults is to weed through the information we've been given, strip away the emotional baggage, make sense of the messages and decode their hidden meanings, and silence the unremitting babble of the ego. It's then—and only then—that we may walk taller, smile brighter, love with unlimited abundance, and actually see beauty when we look in the mirror. It's then that we shine!

A huge part of accessing your unlimited beauty comes through your own healing and self-acceptance. Rising above your past is similar to driving a car: At times you may hit a tight curve in the road and immediately feel the urge to downshift and pull back on the gears, as your ego yells, "Slow down! You can't handle this kind of power!" while it tries to stop you from shining in all your glory. "You're getting just a little too big for your own britches!" it screams. "Who do you think you are?! You can't do this! You've never done it before! You're going to fail!"

But the reality is that where you come from doesn't have any influence on where you're going, any more than the road behind your car has any influence on the highway ahead of it. In fact, those with some of the hardest pasts know that it was all just "driver's training" to enable them to gracefully sail on the journey ahead.

Whenever I feel afraid about something that I have to do, I simply remind myself that everything in my life has prepared me for this moment, and it wouldn't have arrived unless I was ready to handle it. In other words, being on a bumpy and difficult path only means that you have a lot more experience to now handle your vehicle with ease and precision!

As the great writer and psychologist Florida Scott-Maxwell wrote at the age of 84: "You need to claim the events in your life to make yourself yours. When you truly possess all you have been and done, which may take some time, you are fierce with reality."

There Are No Dress Rehearsals

Just as Shakespeare claimed that "all the world's a stage," your life is very similar to a theatrical play: You have a cast of characters, with you being the main one; you have plots, acts, and scenes, filled with dialogue and a climax; and, like all good dramas, you have a theme that you repeat over and over, throughout your life. Each of us performs our specific role because of a payoff (a familiar feeling)—most often for an attempt to receive attention and love. We create our "character" based on our gender, culture, religious values, and family roles, but even more specifically on our *interpretation* of the events we experienced and the beliefs we were taught during our childhood.

Most of us are completely unaware, however, that our life script is the game, so to speak, that we play every day, and we unknowingly become so engrossed in our own story—our life script—that we don't even realize that we're not only creating drama, we've *become* the drama.

Our life script is based on many components, such as watching how our parents and siblings acted and treated us, the messages we heard from them, the suggestions they gave us as to who we were and who we should be, the way they viewed the world and our safety in it, and the messages we were fed from society and the media—as well as the things our parents told us that we could or couldn't do, which are known as *injunctions.*

Injunctions are mostly the "don'ts" we remember hearing, which our childlike ego internalized as:

- "Don't speak."
- "Don't be important."
- "Don't think."

- "Don't be greedy."
- "Don't be demanding."
- "Don't be a child."
- "Don't be stupid."
- "Don't be spoiled."
- "Don't leave me."
- "Don't be needy."
- "Don't embarrass me."
- "Don't act that way."

As adults, many of us will often find ourselves repeating these same messages internally, sometimes grilling ourselves for acting a certain way: "Why am I so stupid? Why do I always do that? If only I could be different, then others would love me more." We basically internalized these injunctions as: "Don't be you!" And maybe we decided that we were "unlovable" or "unimportant," so we began to try to be someone else, in order to make the world like us. Being "ourselves" meant being "wrong." And so, we chose a "mask"—a cover—to hide the things that we were told were no good, without it ever occurring to us that the messages we heard were only someone else's idea of who we should be. Nevertheless, we embraced the messages and created our own childlike perceptions of truth. We created beliefs about who we were and who we'd be in this lifetime.

This calls to mind a story about my client Dorian, who was struggling in her fourth marriage. She couldn't understand why she kept attracting selfish, cold, distant men, when she was so loving and giving herself. After talking for about 15 minutes, zeroing on certain things she said, I asked Dorian if she was an only child. Surprised, she answered yes. I asked her to tell me what her beliefs were about being loved, and what life was like for her while growing up.

My client responded that her parents doted on her, and her needs were always met. To her, love meant that you shower the person you care about with lots of attention and affection.

"Mmm . . . what a wonderful childhood it seems you had," I pointed out. "So to you, being loved means being the center of attention. When people love you, they really need to show it to you through their actions, right?"

Dorian agreed that for her, being loved meant being absolutely adored and catered to in every way. She laughed as she said this, but then added, "But I give just as much attention as I demand!"

"I bet you do!" I smiled. "But how about your husband? What was his childhood like?"

"Oh . . . well, he had 11 siblings and a mother who worked nights as a nurse."

"Wow!" I exclaimed. "I wonder what 'love' means to him?"

I could see that Dorian was getting it: Beliefs aren't right or wrong; they're only perceptions of truth.

Rewrite Your Script

What are *your* beliefs? For example, what were you taught about what was "right and wrong"—your moral code? If you were raised to be a devout Catholic, you may have very different learned beliefs from someone who was raised in a nudist colony. And if your parents were vegetarian Buddhists, you're going to have different learned beliefs from someone who came from Christian cattle ranchers.

If you're interested in seeing how deep-seated your beliefs are, there's a very fascinating tool called the Implicit Association Test (IAT) that shows, through a series of tests, how unconscious associations influence beliefs. The IAT was devised by Anthony G. Greenwald, Mahzarin Banaji, and Brian Nosek, and if you'd like to try a computerized version, visit **www.implicit.harvard.edu/implicit/**. There are tests for age, gender, weight, race, sexuality, and nationality, and you may be shocked to discover that you do carry racist tendencies or are biased against overweight people. The tests won't tell you how to change your beliefs, but they will help you become more aware of the ones you do have. It's important to note that very few of us are able to clearly identify our beliefs and our perceptions of truth unless we've done a lot of work to uncover them. And even then, we'll still see ourselves through our own interpretations. Your "dictionary" is different from mine.

Getting back to our life script, many of us were given a lot fear-driven comments that our parents may have thought were positive motivators. Remarks such as:

- "Make me proud."
- "You can try harder."
- "You're the best—now start acting like it."
- "You'll win next time."
- "I've spent so much time and money helping you succeed . . . I'm counting on you!"

Without realizing it, and usually with good intentions (as most parents certainly don't set out to ruin their children's self-esteem), they unknowingly influenced the tone for our life script. Most often they thought that they were building our confidence or pushing us to succeed, but if their motivation was fear based, then we were raised in an energetic frequency that resonated with pressure and tension—which were perfect conditions for our little egos to grow.

The dynamics also differ from one culture to another. For example, yours may historically contain symbolic themes—stereotypes such as "Germans are evil" while "Jews are virtuous," or the Dutch are like "this" while the Chinese are like "that."

Our scripts also vary with our gender and social status, such as "Little girls are sugar and spice and everything nice, while little boys are frogs and snails and puppy-dog tails." Maybe your parents believed that the rich were smart and hardworking while the poor were dirty and lazy. Or the reverse—that most wealthy people were born with a silver spoon in their mouths and don't have a clue about the "real world."

Our life script is also written on our birth order. Many firstborns often feel more pressure to achieve, while the youngest children might spend their lives grasping at whatever bit of attention they can get. Middle children can either be peacekeepers or rebellious (depending on the firstborn's temperament and will usually be the opposite), while an only child is often a little more self-centered than the rest.

Life scripts also run historically deep, which is why once we understand our family of origin's life script, we can become a part of a wonderful healing for our entire lineage. And just like the saying "Ignorance breeds contempt," our parents passed on many of their own patterns:

- "We Joneses are very proud and don't take handouts."
- "It's not your fault—all the Smith women have a weight problem."
- "The Willards are always in trouble with the law."
- "We've been cursed with bad skin and big noses!"
- "Money is the root of all evil, and we Clarks would rather be poor!"

One of the key things to remember is that you've created your script based on your beliefs, or your attachment to words, experiences, and outcomes. When you begin detaching or separating from the *idea* of "who I am," "who I think I should be," or "who my family is," then you can begin to rewrite your final act from a place of love, understanding, and compassion.

Begin by pulling out your journal and thinking back to the first five years of your life. Psychologists tell us that these crucial years taught us about whether our needs would be met and whether we could trust in the world. What did your first five years teach you? (You must write it down for this to work in your life.)

1. Start by recording your earliest childhood memory. How did it make you feel back then?

2. As you read over this earliest memory, how does it make you feel now?

3. How do you think this memory has set you up in your life? Did it tell you that your needs would be met and that you mattered, or that you were a nuisance and a bother?

4. As you began to age, what did your parents tell or show you about yourself? How about your beauty, your lovableness, your intelligence, your personality, or your ability to succeed?

5. How did you compare to your siblings, parents, or friends? Were you the chubby one or the skinny one, the smart one or the shy one?

6. How does this make you feel now?

7. Can you see how you've created a "theme" or "story" for your life, and how long you've held onto it simply because it's all that you knew?

8. What have you lost in your life by playing out this script?

9. What have you gained in your life by it?

You Are Your Mother's Daughter

Not only does your own past give you amazing lessons to learn from, but when you discover the history of the women who came before you, without judgment or shame, you also begin to really discover the essence of who you are. You see, you're a culmination of your mother, grandmother, and great-grandmother . . . all the way back for generations. Their stories, pain, and successes are so much a part of you that once you understand who you are and where you came from, you'll begin to access an entire library of self-discovery and healing.

The hardest part for most women is facing their own mother-daughter relationship. For some, it's the most meaningful and magical of all relationships, yet it's often the most difficult, too. It's the one we may crave the most, yet it's the one we can also feel the least satisfied by. Nevertheless, even as trying and difficult as your relationship with your mother may have been, it's crucial to realize that it's next to impossible to embrace your own beauty and wonder if you can't see them in the woman who gave birth to you. After all, *you are your mother's daughter.* As Dr. Christiane Northrup shares in her fabulous book *Mother-Daughter Wisdom* (a must-read!): "Every woman who heals herself helps heal all the women who came before her and all those who will come after her."

This reminds me of a conversation I had with a very successful woman who came to me for coaching. Although Anna motivated people every day, teaching them how to face their fears and manifest the miraculous in their lives, she couldn't seem to form a loving relationship with her own mother. However, she was discreet about her personal life, and very few people knew that she and her mom weren't close.

The dilemma my client faced was that she was being presented with a very prestigious award at work, and the CEO of her company had suggested that she invite her entire family, including her parents, to the ceremony. That's when things suddenly went from wonderful to panicked for her.

Although Anna's father had been an alcoholic while she was growing up, he was now clean and sober, and she'd found it in her heart to forgive and accept him. She happily wanted him at her ceremony, but she absolutely did not want her mother to come. Yet since her parents had been married for more than 40 years, she couldn't possibly invite one without the other.

"Crystal, she's never been there for me, so why should I have her there now?" Anna protested.

"I don't know," I replied. "You tell me."

"Everyone at work thinks that things are fine between us, but she just makes me nuts. The way she sits in her house all day, miserable and getting heavier and heavier—all the while looking at me like I think I'm better than her!"

"Hmm," I murmured, waiting for her to continue.

We sat in silence, until I finally said, "Well, Anna, I don't know. There has to be more to this. Really, why don't you want her there?"

After about 30 seconds, she finally spoke. "I'm embarrassed!" she shamefully confessed. "How could I have possibly come from someone so unmotivated and lost as her? Did I tell you that she's like 290 pounds?" she spat. "How can I have her there? Imagine what my staff would think of me!"

Now, Anna was not a hostile or cruel person—in fact, I'd never heard her speak like this before. And in all fairness, her mother *had* been very tough on her, always putting Anna down for being "pretentious, self-absorbed, and a little princess."

There was so much pain between these two that it seemed almost irreparable, but since I believe that what bothers us most about others are the things that really bother us most about ourselves, I told Anna that I thought perhaps her biggest challenge with her mother was really her own fears about herself—that deep down she could one day become her mom.

"Absolutely not!" she exclaimed. "I'm *nothing* like her—nor will I ever be!"

Anna was very motivated, beautiful, and thin, so I gently asked her, "Well, what was your childhood like? How did you feel about yourself?"

She sat in silence, even after I repeated the question . . . and then, slowly and painfully, she began to tell me how she was an extremely overweight child who came from the poorest family in a middle-class neighborhood. Her alcoholic father barely came out of the basement, the other mothers always sneered at Anna's overweight mom, and the kids at school teased her for being fat, singing songs like, "Tubby, Tubby, two-by-four, couldn't fit through the bathroom door."

Anna hated her childhood. And her mother was a constant reminder of it.

I was truly shocked—from all outside appearances, you'd never have guessed that this woman came from such a background. So afraid that the world would judge her based on her mother, this was really about the pain Anna had felt as a little girl, which she'd done everything in her power to erase.

This wasn't about Anna's mom not being there for her (although my client did feel as though she missed out on too much as a child), this was about her own feelings of inadequacy and pain, which she hadn't yet dealt with. The fact remained that Anna wasn't her mother, but she *was* her mother's daughter—and as long as she carried shame about who she came from and who she once was, she'd never be able to truly celebrate herself and be at peace with her mom. She could never "become" until she surrendered and let go what made her so uncomfortable.

I reminded Anna of all this, along with the fact that she was her own person: a beautiful, successful, and happy woman. "I know!" she replied through tears. "And my mom *is* a good woman, too. She's just made some really bad mistakes."

I said that I believed each of us chooses our parents before we even come to this earth, and no matter how difficult, painful, or abusive our childhoods may have been, we must figure out why we would have selected the parents we did. Then I asked what great things Anna's mom had brought into her life: What gifts did my client get and what lessons did she learn from her mother?

Anna slowly began to list some wonderful traits that her mother possessed and then also the qualities she'd gained simply because her mother *didn't* possess them! She started to realize that the childhood she went through was a big part of what has made her into the powerful and extraordinary woman that she is today. "I do love my mom," she admitted. "I know she only did what she knew . . . "

"Love her then," I softly said. "And just remember how extraordinary you are because you came from her—no other mother would have made you, you!"

Anna's greatest fear was that the world would see her as her mother, and then it would judge and condemn her when it discovered her own deep dark secrets of once being overweight and shunned as a child. But once she found the meaning in both of her parents' lives, she went from a position of anger and resentment to one of love and acceptance. The fact is that whatever we focus on in our lives we will manifest—"fear and it will appear!"

When Anna accepted her award two weeks later, with her entire family—including her mom—present, she felt love, acceptance, and peace. And all anyone else saw was my client's beautiful light, shining bright.

Make Peace with Your Past

Do you feel like Anna, ashamed of your past, your parents, or your culture? For those of you who question your own abilities, beauty, and strength—who wonder if you can ever rewrite the script you've been living with—I'd like to remind you that you're the last in your family's line. You're the survivor of survivors, and you have thousands of years of history stored not only in your DNA but also in the legacy of your family's stories. So if you only stay focused on the negative aspects of your history, you'll never be able to access the amazing powers within yourself. I truly believe in my heart of hearts that you can't be at peace with yourself as long as you're at war with your mother. This is a crucial part of your healing . . . but it may be a hard lesson to accept.

Did you know that it was only about a hundred years ago that women in North America were just beginning to persuade men (and perhaps even themselves) that they were more than merely domestic commodities, pieces of property, and birthing machines? They finally demanded that they have rights over their bodies, and that they should be able to vote, hold office, and own land.

Back then, most women were either drudges or dolls, and were in fierce (yet veiled) competition with each other, as their lives and those of their offspring were on the line. The better catch could mean the difference between poverty and illness or prosperity and health. Rosy cheeks signaled vitality, an hourglass figure and full lips exuded fertility, and a woman's hair was her crowning glory. Yet, amazingly, in less than a century, we've had a new stage set for us. Now we can have it all, and, most of us do.

We're the nurturer, lover, caregiver, and breadwinner; the counselor, decorator, sex goddess, and fitness buff; the chauffeur, event planner, midwife, and teacher; the butcher, baker, and candlestick maker. We not only own property, we own multimillion-dollar corporations. And yet so many of us still feel empty. Perhaps that's because our life script was written on the fears and struggles that were passed down to us: from our great-grandmothers to our grandmothers and then to our mothers.

Remember that women have only very recently had any sense of personal power. Most of us are completely unaware of just how oppressed our maternal ancestors were—hundreds, no, *thousands,* of years of patriarchal oppression had left many women drowning in darkness. Even the energetic level, or emotional state, that our own mothers felt during their pregnancies with us have become a huge part of our script, which is why it's so important to embrace our pregnancies with love, reverence, and gratitude. Our babies are counting on us!

Heal Your Legacy

In order to understand your life script, you must understand your mother's. Who is this woman: What did she go through in her life, what beliefs did she develop, and how have her hurts and pains manifested themselves?

What I learned about my own life is that no matter how painful or difficult my teens were (and I had a very tough time), I'd been given a fairy-tale beginning. My mother adored me—I was her precious baby girl, and she whispered that into my infant ears every day. No, she didn't do everything perfectly, for what mother can? But she did the best she could, especially under the circumstances. . . .

Raised in a radically religious home along with her five sisters, my mother knew that she was loved, but she also knew that her father prayed for a son and that her mother desperately wished she could give him one. The entire family lived in a tiny two-bedroom house that overlooked Lake Ontario, and they had very little money.

My mother was a tomboy: Playing sports, running faster than all the boys, climbing higher than the squirrels, and tumbling through the house like an acrobat, she never wanted to be a girl. She'd slick her waist-length blonde hair back into a tight ponytail and then coat it with petroleum jelly, hoping to perhaps resemble Gene Kelly, Elvis Presley, or Marlon Brando.

As she hit puberty, however, my mother's body started to change, so she rinsed out the Vaseline and began sneaking on makeup, using car windows on the way to school as her mirror (being sure to scrub it off before she got home). Everywhere she went, people stared—especially boys. Her father introduced her to everyone as his "most beautiful daughter, Donna," even in front of his other girls. She was spectacular, and everyone knew it.

One night when she was 14, my mother was coerced into a car by two older men as she walked home. "It's too late and dark for you to be out alone," they said. "We have daughters close to your age, so jump in—we'll give you a ride."

Hesitantly, she asked to see ID. Everything within her was screaming to just keep walking, but she'd been taught to listen to her elders. Her instincts were right: As soon as she climbed in, one held her captive while the other drove. My mother was taken to a deserted area north of Toronto, where both men raped her and then left her on the side of an old country road. She'd never smelled cigarettes or alcohol before, and it wasn't until much later that she understood they were both intoxicated.

Bleeding and alone in the dark, she tried to wrap her ripped clothes around her and started the very long walk home. But as she got closer, she realized that she couldn't go home—after all, she never should have gotten in that car in the first place! Instead, she went to her boyfriend's house and broke down sobbing. His father then took her to the police station.

Devastated, my grandparents showed up at the station, where they sat crying, listening as my mother recounted the tale with graphic detail. The police had to know everything. . . . As she lay on the ground in front of the car after they'd bashed her head against the passenger door, Mom had kept focused on the license plate, and she was able to recite it to the officers with perfect precision.

After the police station came the hospital—rape kit, blinding bright lights, cold gurney, strange doctors and nurses—where she lay naked once again, terrified and invaded twice in one night.

Once she'd climbed into the car with her parents, her father quietly yet firmly told her that she wouldn't be testifying in court and that no one was ever to know about this. "It is never to be discussed again," he flatly said. He wanted to protect her and the family name, so that was that.

My mother crawled into bed that night and told only her closest sister what had happened. No one else would ever know—the family secret would be safe—and the shame overtook her. She later found out that the men were both fathers and did indeed have daughters her age. They'd been coming home from a baseball game the night they spotted her walking alone. They each received six months probation for abducting and raping a 14-year-old virgin. That was 1964—women had no *real* rights.

The following year was a blur, and many days my mother would swim out as far as she could into the dark and stormy waters of Lake Ontario. But no matter how far she went or how tired she was, something inside her always made her turn around and fight her way back to shore. She was a survivor.

At age 17, Mom compounded her shame by coming home pregnant. After she was married off to my father, a guy who drove a fast car, wore stunning suits, and came from the "right side of the tracks," her parents crossed their fingers, hoping that he'd give her the life she deserved. But my mom had big dreams, and raising babies wasn't one of them. Nevertheless, my dad was a charismatic and handsome young guy who had some pretty big dreams of his own. Together, they were going to have it all, and we kids were little replicas of them.

Jeff, my older brother, did everything with my dad, while I stuck beside my mom in our little sheltered fairy-tale life. When I was seven, my sister, Tiffany, came along. Apparently, it was quite a surprise to Mom, who was just beginning to have hope that she'd soon have a life outside of us. My stay-at-home mother drilled into me that getting married and having babies was *not* the life I was meant to live, yet she resigned herself to staying at home awhile longer. She was a very good mom.

Then one day after finding some suspicious letters in my father's briefcase, her world collapsed, and her scorn grew. How could this man betray her? She'd devoted her life to him and his kids! He denied that he was having an affair and begged her for forgiveness, but she wasn't going for it. With no chance for reconciliation, my mother grasped at whatever possibility of freedom and success she could hold on to. She didn't intentionally plan to throw the babies out with the bathwater, but she was hurt and angry. We'd *all* ruined her life—her hopes and dreams—at least that's how I felt.

Mom got a job at a local gym and was going to prove to the world that she was somebody. Within a few years, she owned that gym and became one of Canada's top female bodybuilders. We kids were hurt and angry, looking at her as though she were to blame for all our pain. Couldn't she just forgive Dad? Couldn't we just keep our home, our cottage, our boat, our Ski-Doos, our father . . . *our lives?* But children seemed to cramp her style, and she was done being a mother.

I ended up moving out on my own by age 15, after being repeatedly raped over the course of the summer by a male relative of one of Mom's new boyfriends. It would take 20 years to begin healing the pain because I was hurt and angry and only felt frustration and pain whenever I was around her. It truly wasn't until I got into my 30s, after having my own children and going through a painful divorce, that a dramatic shift in me occurred. I started looking at my mom in a new light, understanding her in a way I never had before. Yes, she'd made some poor choices, but *why* had she?

The more I started to make meaning out of my mother's life, the more I began to look at the world through her eyes. Soon I began to see her anger, *and my own,* as pure sadness. I started to welcome her for all her wonderful, crazy ways (because she has so many) and overlooking the things that had always made *me* crazy. By doing so, I was finally beginning to embrace the magic of my mother. It was time to put the past behind us.

Interestingly, as that happened, a shift in my relationship with her also occurred. As I began to treat her differently, she began to treat *me* differently, and it was suddenly so easy to see my smile and mannerisms in hers, and to thank her for my persistence, charisma, and passionate personality. I think that she was also beginning to see the love and kindness that others had seen in me all these years. The bottom line was that as long as I stayed focused on what was wrong, I could never see what was so right! So I stared to claim the right to be me by honoring her. At the same time, I was teaching my own two daughters how to treat me with love and respect.

We are our mother's daughters, and once we properly revere the beauty and strength of these women, we begin to sit taller, walk stronger, and shine with a brighter glow. There is beauty in everyone—no matter what our situation, no matter what our history, no matter what our pain or challenges—and forgiveness, compassion, understanding, and love will heal all. Love can move mountains, and that is true power.

It's time to release the old patterns and the beliefs that you've been carrying since birth. By understanding that your parents (as well as your siblings and other family members) have unknowingly influenced the way you think, react, talk, and deal with stress, you'll begin to notice your own patterns. This will help you break the ones that are holding you back, while embracing the ones that can catapult your life forward.

What's most important to realize is that "the blame game" is a sport for victims (who, interestingly enough, resonate at an extremely low frequency), and to transcend beauty we must never be this way. Instead, we must "name it, claim it, grieve it, and release it." Blaming Mom or Dad—or anyone else, for that matter—is pointless and actually self-destructive. The ego lives in the past and must blame someone, so it looks to be offended and holds on to resentment. As long as we live in blame, we don't have to take responsibility for our lives, so we can use that blame as an excuse not to demand the most for ourselves now.

In order to move forward and to recognize the beauty and wonder of yourself, you must be willing to become completely accountable to yourself and your life script. Once you "own your story," you'll be able to begin rewriting a new, more beautiful future! So take a few minutes and write the answers down to the following questions in your journal:

1. What was your mother's childhood like—what did she go through?

2. How did she take care of herself when you were young?

3. Was she comfortable and at ease with her reflection? Did she like living in a woman's body?

4. Does she (or did she) see herself as a beautiful, strong, successful, lovable woman; or as a victim; a martyr; or perhaps even just unlucky or unloved? What theme did you learn from her?

5. What about Dad—what messages did he send to you about Mom? About you? How did he view women in general?

In order for you to act out this amazing play called "life" with beauty, confidence, and love, you must be willing to let go of the old beliefs that are no longer serving you—the old self-sabotaging messages. You need to figure out the theme you keep repeating and understand the payoff you get by creating your dramas. Each time your mind begins to try to retrace its old familiar steps, remind yourself that *you have to let it go.* Letting go is a choice, and once you see how truly easy it is to make that choice, you'll find the process getting easier and easier.

Again, using your journal, answer the following questions:

1. What are five wonderful qualities that your mother brought to your life? What have you gained by having these qualities?

2. What are five wonderful qualities that your father brought to your life? What have you gained by having these qualities?

3. Thinking of these things, how does it make you feel about yourself right now?

4. What are five negative things that your mother brought to your life?

5. What are five negative things that your father brought to your life?

6. Thinking of these things, how does it make you feel?

The secret that spiritually enlightened people have learned is to take the negative things—the pain, fear, and emotional roadblocks—and turn them into positive. In other words, how can you look at all of your life's experiences and make meaning of why they happened the way they did?

Answer the following questions in your journal:

1. How have the negative experiences in your life created positives in you? That is, how can you find the gifts in the experiences of your life? How have they made you a stronger person?

2. Do you think that you'd be the person you are today had you not gone through everything that you've been through?

3. If you were to write out ten words to describe your life, what would they be? (Not a sentence but rather one word, followed by another word, and then another, and so on.)

4. From age one to five was the "first act" of your life. From age 6 to 18 was Act II, and from then to the present day has been Act III. What's the final act of your life going to be? (Make it a good one!)

The Thread Sewn into the Fabric of You

Most of us don't know who our grandmothers were, let alone our great-grandmothers. How did they meet their husbands? What were their childhoods like? How many siblings did they have? How long were they married? How did they die—and more important, how did they live?

Not long ago, I took my daughters to visit my grandmother, whom I absolutely adore. She's 91 now and has really aged in the last ten years since Grandpa died. When we arrived, she was sitting in her rocking chair, alone in her bedroom at the nursing home. Her eyes were shut, and she was facing a wall. As I touched her shoulder, she barely moved, and when I leaned down to murmur in her ear that I'd arrived, she sat almost motionless, with her eyes still closed. Finally, she whispered a hello.

After a few minutes, she opened her eyes and asked how my mom was doing. Sadly, I didn't have much to share because I hadn't seen much of her either. Grandma shook her head, a tear rolled down her cheek, and her eyes closed again.

It's important that you have the support you need, especially during this time of rediscovery, so please visit my message forum at **www.crystalandrus.com.** I post on it daily, and it has proven to be one of the greatest Internet sites for sharing and healing. When we feel totally and completely comfortable to speak our truth, reach out for a shoulder to cry on, and let other nurturing and caring women into our lives for support and friendship, we begin trusting in ourselves. We can only heal what we're willing to face *and to share.* The truth shall set us free.

If you need extra support, honor yourself by finding a good therapist or counselor. Also, feel free to contact me for personal coaching—even a few sessions can shine some powerful light on you. (For more details, just go to my Website and just click on the "Coach on Call" link.)

The truth is that for most of my life, I was an "island"—too afraid to let anyone play on my beach. I could help anyone, but I never dared to reveal the "shameful" stories of my own life. However, I came to realize that we're all so much more alike than we know, and that no matter how wonderful someone's life may seem, we all need support when we're down.

As Wendy, a member of the forum, wrote after retreating into her shell for a while and then rejoining us again: "I'm slowly learning to embrace the friendships and support [of the gals on the message forum] instead of running and hiding when I fail. After all, having hands that help you up after you fall feels so much better than sitting in the hole alone! It's so much better to be building sand castles together."

The secret to being loved and accepted is to reach out for support. This is the only step we have to take—the rest effortlessly comes to us. When we share our gifts with the world, God smiles down on us, and it raises the entire level of human consciousness. But only you can reach out and take our hands. . . .

Kneeling down in front of her wheelchair, I took her hands in mine—and then I reached out to my daughters, joining us in a small circle. I asked my grandmother what her mother's name was, and she answered that it was Janet. I then asked what her grandmother's name was. She couldn't remember at first, but then said that she thought it was Marion, the same as hers. I then asked her what her great-grandmother's name was. Shaking her head, Grandma couldn't recall it, but then she murmured that she sees them *all* in her dreams all the time now, and that she'd rather sleep and be with them than sit awake, waiting. . . .

I closed my eyes and said each of my foremothers' names out loud and told my grandmother that all the power and strength of her mother, grandmother, and great-grandmother lies within her—"All that strong Scottish will!"

She softly laughed.

"And all that power also lies in my mother and in me, and now I've passed it down to my girls, too." I continued.

I opened my eyes, looked at my daughters, and said, "Madelaine, Julia, I want you to always remember that all the strength, beauty, and power of Mommy, Grandma, and Great-Grandma," squeezing Grandma's hand tighter, "that of Janet, your great-great grandma; and Marion, your great-great grandmother; lies within you both. There's nothing you can't do! And anytime you feel afraid or unsure, you just call out our names and we'll be with you. All of us! You never have to be afraid because you're never alone."

Instantly, my grandmother opened her eyes, and she quietly asked if my mother thought that way, too. We care so much what our daughters think of us, don't we? In that moment, I suddenly felt so aware that although all daughters need to know that their mommies love them, all mommies need to know that their daughters love them, too.

As I sat talking with my grandmother, I discovered so much about her life—for example, she didn't even know when her own mother was pregnant. In a patriarchal culture, discussing pregnancy was considered disgraceful, or at best, inappropriate. Nevertheless, one by one, many babies appeared in my grandmother's home in less than 15 years, without any warning or family discussion. Nursing was to be done only in private, usually in a back room. "Not that that really mattered," Grandma told me, "as most women were told that their own breast milk was second to formula anyway." (Another myth created by male doctors to disempower us even more.)

I can only imagine how degraded and alone my great-grandmother must have felt, knowing that she was to keep her pregnancies hidden or that having girls was a disappointment to her husband. I realized that she only did what she knew and that she must have been so strong and mighty to have raised 11 children in a time without running water, plumbing, or even a man around the house much of the time. She developed beliefs that had been passed down to her, and she naturally instilled these same messages in her own children. And my grandmother—the eldest girl of the 11 kids—was her mother's daughter.

When Grandma was 14, she and her family climbed off a train at Union Station in Toronto. Eleven children and two adults had taken the long and arduous journey from Scotland across the Atlantic and into Canada, sleeping in three tiny cots for more than a week. After riding across the country on the Canadian Pacific railroad, they finally walked out into their new city, wearing the only good set of clothes they owned and carrying a few bags between them all. They were met by a Mountie, riding a huge horse, who asked Grandma's father, "Sunday-school class?"

"Nope, they're all mine!" he replied. There they were: 11 children all under the age of 16, with little food, no money, and no place to go. But they had hope and courage . . . they were survivors.

Finding food and shelter for them all was more than my great-grandfather had bargained for, so my grandma and her two oldest brothers were sent off to live and work on different farms miles outside of the city. Grandma received no money for her 16-hour workdays, but she was given the basics—toilet paper, soap, and a bit of food, which she could then send back to her family.

Within no time, the people she worked for showed their displeasure with the deal and often refused to give her anything to send back. Grandma may have been only 14, but this was not going to work in her book—they'd made a deal, and she'd fulfilled her side of the bargain. She decided that she'd report these people to the government if they didn't treat her with more respect and honor, and she told them so! My great-grandfather tried to hush my feisty 14-year-old granny, but nothing would stop her. She was Scottish and tough, and she was going to stand up for what was right. She was a hard worker, and the family she worked for didn't want to lose her. Within the month, her family began to receive their sundries.

As typified by Grandma, I came from strong women. No, they didn't hug or cry much or say "I love you," yet everything in their being was about family, love, and taking care of each other.

"I knew my mum loved me," Grandma told me as we sat and talked that day. "She didn't have to say it—she showed it." And because of that, Grandma didn't know how to say it to her daughters, either. Nor did my mom know how to say it to me. The river runs deep. . . .

As I left my grandmother that day, I vowed to find out more about the women who set my life into motion, and to honor the strength, passion, fortitude, and beauty that they all possessed . . . and that *I* now possessed, too!

I also made a pact with myself that we'd all start spending more time together. Three weeks later, on Mother's Day, my mother, my sister and her kids, and my daughters and I went to visit Grandma. She looked the youngest I'd seen her in ten years.

What about you? What kind of women did you come from? What are your grandmothers' names? How about your great-grandmothers and your great-great-grandmothers? If you don't know, *learn them!* And anytime you feel alone or afraid, call out their names. You'll feel an energy and power rise within you, as I promise that your ancestors are never far away.

I came from strong women who had to fight for everything they ever got. My great-grandmother was a survivor, and my grandmother followed perfectly in her wake. My mother . . . well, she's the epitome of "survivor," and I was carrying along in the same vein. But then I stopped and asked myself it that's what I wanted . . . and if I wanted my children to be survivors, too.

You see, survivors have to claw their way out of the darkness; in fact, the very word denotes pain and suffering. No, I didn't want to be a survivor, and I didn't want that for my girls either. I wanted to be a *"thrivor,"* one who thrived throughout life. I wanted my daughters to see that you don't have to live from a place of pain, victimization, worry, and fear. Now, don't get me wrong—I love and honor the women I came from, and I'm thankful that they fought and pushed and clawed. But I realized that it was time to shift to a higher resonance, to live as though I knew with 100 percent certainty that my needs would always be met; that my safety would always be preserved; and that abundance, love, compassion, and understanding was my right. I didn't want to fight for it. I simply wanted to claim it . . . be it . . . know it . . . and live it! And I wanted my girls to know that their future was guaranteed to be magnificent.

It was time to heal my legacy and to whisper out into the darkness, "Thank you, Donna. Thank you, Marion. Thank you, Janet. Thank you to all my guardian angels . . . *my grandmothers.* The fight is over, and we can all rest now, knowing that our bloodline is strong, powerful, and truly at peace."

Be humble for you are made of earth.
Be noble for you are made of stars.
— Serbian Proverb

Love the Skin You're In

I remember my mother telling me when I was a teenager that I should never let a man see me without makeup on . . . not even my own husband. She told me that the mistress always gets treated better than the wife and to always be sexy for your man. Sad, isn't it? My poor mom!

It's amazing now, looking back, because I think that from a young age I believed that when I painted my eyes up like a cat's, I turned into the woman I needed to be. When I felt sexy, I felt powerful—and I guess I'd somehow equated sex with power, power with beauty, and beauty with makeup. I knew that when my eyelashes were coated in mascara and my skin glowed with shimmering powder, I was attractive. My lips were shiny and luscious with gloss, and my blemishes were hidden under foundation. Men stared, and I felt important. But I also knew that every night when I washed away my cover, my confidence went down the drain, too.

Who was I without makeup? And why was I so afraid to have someone see me without it on?

I've now discovered that makeup wasn't the problem, but rather, it was that I believed that without it I'd be inadequate, ugly, and even worse—that someone might discover who I really was. *And who was that?*

Dare to Walk Naked

Our mask is the thing that we believe defines us, protects us, and makes us more acceptable to the world (or maybe it makes the world more acceptable to us). It's our false courage, the covering we create to protect ourselves from the world. But what we often don't even realize is that what once protected us has now become our captor. Most of us are unaware that the thing we think we need most is actually our weakest link—our Achilles' heel, so to speak.

I know that I often use the saying "fear and it will appear," but it's the truth. The things we end up spending so much time trying to hide from the world end up becoming what the world actually sees—that is, we actually manifest our greatest fears into our reality. So the more I obsessed about looking perfect and hiding my "flaws" from the world, the more I noticed them, the more I talked about them, the more I worked on fixing them, and the more I seemed to attract others who felt they had the right to point them out to me.

Think about some of the people you know, such as the fanatical housekeeper or obsessive organizer in your family: She's so worried that the world will see her "faults" that she spends her life trying to be perfect and in control, yet anyone with half a brain can clearly see that she's not at peace with herself. Or how about the aging woman who's terrified that the world will see that she's losing her youthful beauty and gaining a little bit of weight: She's so afraid to grow old gracefully that she stays stuck in a time warp, dressing younger and sexier than she should, looking totally ridiculous, and becoming the very thing she feared most.

What's *your* mask? Is it your education, your five-dollar words, or your fancy car? Some women use designer outfits, immaculate hair, and fake nails, while others bury themselves under bottles of wine or mounds of ice cream. Many wealthy people hide behind their possessions, while most bodybuilders or fitness fanatics pose behind their muscles or sculpted physiques.

Then there are those at the opposite end of the spectrum—those who've given up. They hide behind the mask of comfort and complacency, as they walk around in sloppy clothes and eat unhealthy food, too lazy to take the time to bother with themselves. Terrified to really live their dreams, they stay stuck, convinced that this is "as good as it gets." Their mask is one of indifference.

Your mask could be something as silly as the coffee and cigarette you "must" have before you can face the world, or something as serious as the drinks or pills you take to ease you through life's natural ups and downs. Revealing what you hide behind is about letting go of the idea of who you're supposed to be and just *becoming* her. It's about self-acceptance, being comfortable in your own skin, and discovering that your mask is really what's been holding you back from shining in all your glory. For once you surrender and face yourself without any facades or armor, you'll come to know true power . . . and transcend beauty!

Ask yourself the following:

- Can you go to the mall without wearing makeup?
- Can you walk in front of your lover without clothes, in the light, and feel totally comfortable?
- Can you look at *all* of your body parts with comfort and ease?
- How much time in a day do you spend on your appearance?

- Can you walk by mirrors without looking at your reflection, or get out of your car without checking the rearview mirror first?

- Is hair just hair or does it define you? In other words, could you cut off your locks to just a pixie cut and still feel sexy?

- Do you have to put on lipstick the minute you're done eating in a restaurant?

- Can you look at your bare hands, without polish, and see beauty and strength?

- What about when traveling—can you go with a light bag filled with just your essentials?

- Are you comfortable at the beach wearing only a bathing suit?

- Could you feel beautiful in a developing country without the luxuries from home?

- If you were to tear up your credit cards, downsize your home, and drive an older car, would you feel less successful?

- Do you try to keep up with the Joneses or put yourself in debt trying to give the perfect Christmas gifts?

- Does buying things make you feel wealthy and thriving?

- How would you feel if you no longer possessed your jewelry or handbags?

- What if someone dropped by your home and it was an absolute mess—would you feel comfortable inviting them in for coffee?

The only way to become your most beautiful and authentic self is to actually just peel your mask off and do exactly what you're most afraid of. In my case, the idea of being seen without makeup (even just a touch of mascara) was unbearable. Yet if I think back to my learned beliefs, it shouldn't surprise me . . . after all, I learned that a woman was only beautiful when she was glamorous and sexy, and I saw it from the time I could see! My mother would strut her stuff—done up "to the max"—everywhere we went, even to the beach. I really don't think I've *ever* seen her with her face completely scrubbed clean. Consequently, as a little girl I felt like a "plain Jane" (a little geek), and I ached for the day that people would take notice of me the way they did my mom.

Now, this is not intended to put my mother down. She honestly believes that every woman should wear makeup and that those who don't must not love themselves enough to take care of themselves. This is her truth . . . but for many years, it became *my* truth, too. It didn't matter who told me I was beautiful without makeup on—in my mind, that was an impossibility. The only solution was to redefine my beliefs, so I finally dared myself to "walk naked"! I decided that I wouldn't wear any makeup for one week. And the catch was that I had to do all the things I normally would have done: meetings, luncheons, dinner dates, and whatever was scheduled for that week.

If you're not a makeup person, this may sound ridiculous, but keep in mind that you have a mask, too. It could be your money that you hide behind, or even your religion. It could be your nonchalant attitude (which is secretly shrouded in fear), your shyness, or your self-righteousness. The point is not what mask *I* wore, it's that our masks are all about hiding our "real selves" from the world.

Anyway, the first day out, I slipped on a baseball hat, pulled on some sweats, and snuck out my door. *Sunglasses!* I thought. *Yes, large ones that can hide most of my face! I'll need monstrous black sunglasses!* I rushed to get myself the largest pair I could find.

Next was grocery shopping: As I crept through the aisles, I hung my head low, avoiding eye contact with everyone. I truly could not have been any other way, and it was so painful. All that kept going through my head was, *God, I just hope no one recognizes me.*

No one did. In fact, no one noticed me at all. Not a single man glanced my way! Now that the world could really see me, I told myself that my beliefs were right: *See, I'm really not pretty after all!*

As my day went on, I noticed how differently I was treated. I guess the truth is that I was being treated like a "regular woman," without any of the perks I'd grown accustomed to. Men didn't give me any attention—not that I would have really noticed, since I couldn't look their way either. It suddenly seemed so apparent to me that my entire being depended upon attention in order to feel good.

The next day, I was meeting a friend for lunch, so I dressed a little nicer, did my hair, but still wore a somewhat subdued outfit. I needed to blend in as much as possible. When I first arrived, I sat in my vehicle for few minutes and wondered if putting Vaseline on my lips counted as makeup—I mean, technically, it wasn't lip gloss! *Why was I doing this to myself?*

Once in the restaurant, I choose the darkest corner, closest to the back. I got there early on purpose, and when my friend arrived, she was shocked. Her surprised look made me cringe, and I sank lower into the chair. "Crystal Andrus, I have never seen you on time for anything!" she squealed. "I think you're actually early!" She laughed and sat down.

There was no mention of my face yet, so I immediately began pointing out my horrid appearance—my blemishes, wrinkles, and all my flaws—figuring that if I brought attention to them, she wouldn't have to. As I explained my experiment, she smiled . . . and then moved right along into the story she'd been dying to tell me for weeks.

My bleak face didn't seem to cause the scene that I'd imagined it would. In fact, my friend said that she didn't see much of a difference. *How could that be? Well, she's only trying to be nice,* I figured.

It was great to see her, though, and by the end of lunch we'd gotten to laughing so hard that I accidentally forgot and took off my sunglasses, to wipe away my streaming tears. She never said anything, nor did I—we were having too much fun to notice. Some men in the restaurant looked over and smiled, and one even sent us a drink, speculating that it must have been one of our birthdays. The waitress said he'd commented that he'd never seen such beautiful and vivacious women!

As my friend and I smiled and lifted our glasses to say thank you, I suddenly remembered my naked face. My smile quickly faded, as my embarrassment consumed me. I quickly put my shades back on and sank another four inches into my chair.

And then something occurred to me: When I'd forgotten that I didn't have any makeup on and acted with the same confidence and exuberance as when I was wearing it, the world treated me just the same. But when I felt ugly and hid my head with shame, the world treated me like a wallflower.

Was it really the case that all these years I believed I couldn't be pretty without cosmetics, so I created a world that produced that reality? With makeup I walked with confidence; without it I avoided eye contact and direct discourse. How could I have possibly exuded vitality and beauty when I felt so low?

For the rest of the week, my experiment got easier and easier, until I actually began to feel great without "my face" on. There's a saying, "Fake it till you make it"—and it truly works!

On the following Monday, as I got ready to head off to work, I put on my makeup with freedom. I was okay with it *and* without it. (My lips did look fantastic with gloss, but they were pretty good without it, too!) Now, don't get me wrong: Just as there's a distinction between care and adoration, there's also one between ease and negligence. Negligence doesn't serve you any differently than adoration does.

So let me reiterate that I'm not suggesting makeup is something to avoid—on the contrary! Once you see the inner beauty that you already possess, then lipstick becomes an instrument to celebrate your mouth, rather than cover it. Teeth whitener can be a means to make them as bright as they were meant to be, bronzer can accentuate those glorious cheekbones, and mascara can simply honor your eyes. In other words, they're just tools to enhance what's already there . . . should you want to use them. For once you love yourself *for you,* these things simply become part of the rituals used in that celebration.

It made perfect sense to recite my "makeup experience" to my client Karen, who hadn't been on a date for nearly ten years. "Oh, my God, I get it!" she exclaimed. "Even though I'm the complete opposite of you, I see how my mask is holding me back. I never do my hair, barely wear any makeup, and like to walk around in sweats. I don't wear dresses and wouldn't dream of acting flirtatious. Maybe that's why I never attract men, yet I have tons of them as friends. I'm totally comfortable with my 'athletic side,' but I'm not with my 'sexy side' Maybe I use my complacency as my mask."

For me, attracting male admirers was effortless, but I actually used to believe that men and women could *not* be friends. And here was Karen, who was completely at ease with her "athletic side" (as she called it) but not with her femininity or sexuality, and she only attracted male friends.

I asked what the craziest thing she could do to evoke the goddess within her would be, and she said to buy a sexy dress and high heels, and go out dancing with her girlfriends. One week later, she told me she'd been asked to go out on her first date in years!

Let's explore masks further. Ask yourself the following:

- Are you comfortable dressing up—sliding on stockings, wearing high heels, and celebrating the goddess within?

- Do you use bath oils, light candles, and honor your femininity?

- Do you judge others who buy expensive perfumes, designer clothes, or sparkling diamonds?

- Do you honor your "temple" daily by eating healthy food, exercising, and meditating?

- Do you shrink from the limelight, preferring to blend in with the background?

- If invited to a five-star restaurant, do you embrace the experience and enjoy the cuisine?
- Are you able to freely compliment others and receive praise without blushing or feeling unworthy?
- Do you take the time to fix yourself up when going out?
- Would you spend the money on a dress you really wanted or a necklace you think is beautiful?
- Do you embrace your femininity and sexuality?
- Do you honor all other women and accept them for their femininity and sexuality, too?

Detachment comes from embracing the fact that nothing *is* or *is not;* that nothing owns you, nor do you own it; that all things are just that—*things*—they're neither good nor bad; and that you alone, without your mask, are just fine.

Once you get that your strength and beauty come exclusively from within—and can never come from something outside of yourself—you can actually begin to celebrate and honor yourself . . . with and without your facade. While wearing a mask is sometimes fun, until you can walk naked, it will be your hindrance—for if you think you need it, then, sadly, you do. That's because the only time you will feel even remotely beautiful or slightly powerful is when you hide behind something.

If you want to control what you are, you'll never resonate at a frequency of beautiful bliss. Once you know which self you're serving, you'll gently and happily realize that lipstick and mascara are not the enemy, but rather great friends that you can have fun with when you choose to!

Sophia Loren, one of the most beautiful women in world, eloquently said that "nothing makes a woman more beautiful than the belief that she is beautiful." She's absolutely right . . . but for more reasons than she probably knew. You see, when you innately believe that you're beautiful, your energetic frequency skyrockets to a resonance of intense luminosity. Your energies align with the universal energetic frequency of beauty, and all who see you will note that and be mesmerized by your breathtaking power.

However, if you truly believe that you're ugly—that your legs are gross or that your skin is old and wrinkled—then no matter how desperately you try to project beauty, you won't. No amount of makeup can ever give it to you, as your energetic frequency will align with the low, dark, and repelling emotions of shame and self-loathing. Even more frustrating is that you attract what you're emitting.

Whenever the inner struggle arises within you (where you feel afraid to face the world without your mask), then simply remind yourself that you can't serve two masters: the ego, who wants you to believe that you aren't enough; and the soul, who simply knows that you're already Divine. The easiest way to discover what mask you're hiding behind is to make a list of the things you love most about yourself and your life—all your possessions, personal attributes, and qualities—and then ask yourself, "If I were to lose these things, would I still feel okay about myself?"

Release and surrender to what is, without the fear that it isn't enough. When you do, you'll know freedom . . . and you'll shine in all your glory!

Tame the Beast

When we resist what *is* and try to make something what we *believe it should be,* we swim against the very current of who we are. Life seems difficult: We feel tired and drained, create drama, fight with others, become indignant, and force situations to go our way. But when we're living the life our soul innately knows is right, and when we honor ourselves exactly as we are, we feel truly balanced—emotionally, physically, mentally, hormonally, and spiritually. We're at ease, we like who we are, and we resonate with authentic power and beauty. (Continued on page 67 . . .)

You Have to *See* It Before You Can *Be* It

Throughout my life, I've often wondered if I willed things into being or if I truly saw them before they happened. There have been so many times, from childhood to this day, that I've closed my eyes and seen myself in a situation, only to have it happen exactly the way I imagined it would—weeks, months, or sometimes even years later.

Was this my intuition lighting the way for me, or merely me manifesting my intentions into my reality? Was I co-creating my experiences using the power of meditation, visualization, and taking action?

Well, I believe it was all of these things—and I believe that we all have this ability!

Before Michael Jordan takes a shot, he's already seen that basketball swishing through the hoop, and before Tiger Woods makes a putt, he's already watched the golf ball drop into the hole. In other words, if you can't see yourself somewhere—if you can't close your eyes and envision that you've already "arrived"—then how do you think you'll ever get there?

You have to see it before you can be it. Whatever your mind sees, it will believe, and it will be sure to make it your reality. This can work both positively and negatively in your life: If you believe that you're destined to be sick, you will be. If you see the world as essentially good, it will be good right back. If you're condemning and judgmental (even if on the surface you act righteous and wonderful), you'll experience the world as a negative place. If you innately believe that you're blessed, than you will be. If you send love out to everyone in your life, at all times, then your relationships will be fulfilling and you'll feel loved. If you give off anger or indifference, life will feel painful and complicated. If you believe that making money is difficult, it will be, and vice versa.

Fear attracts scarcity and lack, but if you give with an open and generous heart, you'll always live with abundance. If you feel hurt, fearful, insecure, angry, resentful, or unsure, you're going to send off energy that attracts those same low-calibrating emotions in others. Or, conversely, if you think joyous, compassionate thoughts, you'll organically and effortlessly attract beautiful people into your life. But this all works on the deepest levels: You can't pretend with a painted-on smile and an unconvincing tone in your voice.

If you want to take a different path, make a change in your life, heal a disease, forgive someone who's hurt you, get that promotion, or even lose weight, you must begin to manifest your reality with the power of your mind. Once you've set your intentions, you must take action. *Nothing will change until you change!* Words and even noble emotion will not suffice—it's in the labor of the body and mind. It's effort, discipline, and focus that separate the "talkers" from the "doers." For example, no matter how much I meditated on being a published author, I still needed to sit down at my computer for three to four hours each night and write the book. I needed to knock on doors and search for those who would help me.

Action, combined with intention, is the secret of success. Whatever you focus on, you will become . . . the secret is making sure that your intentions are soul-driven. That is, they must be affirming in intent, good for all parties involved, and driven with energetically authoritative and optimistic words. Your thoughts and prayers can't be: "Oh, no, I'm worried about this. I hope it will work out, but you know, I've seen this same thing before and it didn't. Yet I have faith. I'll pray!" Honestly, you're better off not sending any energy to a situation than to send negative thoughts out there—remember, whatever you focus on, you give power to.

Be very selective of the words you choose and the thoughts you think, as there's a powerful distinction between positive and negative. For example, the word *striving* signifies an enthusiastic intent, whereas *struggling* infers pessimistic. *Observant* implies an optimistic awareness, while *suspicious* denotes a distrustful outlook. Comments such as "He destroyed me," "My head is killing me," "I'm starving," "I hate these family functions," "I've given up trying to win them over," "There's never really a good time," "I'm a positive person, but she's so negative," and "This disease is deadly, but I'm going to try to fight it" all give power to the very thing you don't want in your life, or in your body. Your words just end up making it stronger and yourself weaker.

As hokey as it may initially feel, by learning to rephrase your words to align with your desires, rather than your current perceptions, you'll begin to manifest the miraculous. Focus on whatever it is you want to accomplish by closing your eyes and envisioning it unfolding in your mind's eye. See yourself in exactly the way you dream it will be. Breathe it in, feel it, and stay focused on it!

Resistance to what is blocks the flow of life because it steals away our power and ultimately leaves us feeling weak, unsure, and afraid. When we fight a circumstance, a person, or a feeling within ourselves, we unknowingly give away our energy because we produce so much stress. That stress then takes over and robs us of any bit of beauty we have left.

Resistance can happen in almost any forum in our lives: We resist having fun, moving forward in our lives, or developing new relationships. We resist the act of forgiveness, especially forgiving ourselves for something we might have done when we were younger, and we resist letting go of past grievances, playing them over and over in our mind. We resist being in the moment, letting go of old wounds, or embracing the future with faith. We resist dancing, playing, creating, eating, loving, and learning. We resist our bodies, our beauty, and our own feelings. We resist ourselves for fear of looking conceited, self-absorbed, or even worse—silly or stupid. Maybe we even resist life itself, simply out of fear of finding something new and exciting. What might that mean? Well, perhaps it's easier to stay miserable than to be wrong or to have to do something about your misery.

Remind yourself that this resistance is in and from you, *not from the world and not from God!* This is a fear that your mind-made self believes you need to hold on to—your ego is too terrified to let it go and yet too terrified to let it be. But instead of rejecting this part of yourself, you can simply ask, "What is this resistance trying to teach me?"

You see, resistance confronts you with the unhealthiest parts of yourself—those that judge, condemn, blame, worry, fear, and hate—the parts that must be uncovered and healed in order for you to feel fully "whole" . . . to become the "I am." Always remember that the struggle you're experiencing is simply the voice of your ego trying to stop you from evolving, and you can use this feeling of resistance in your body to learn valuable lessons about you and what you fear most. Once you heal this fearful and hurtful aspect of your consciousness, the resistance will leave you—permanently.

The Voice of the Ego

I'd been doing soul coaching for quite some time, but it wasn't until my dear friend Colette Baron-Reid, internationally renowned intuitive counselor and the author of the fantastic new book *Remembering the Future,* taught me something very profound that I really understood the power of the ego. At the time, I was going through a difficult situation in my life and was feeling very afraid and totally unsure of how to handle things. Colette asked, "Why are you having such a hard time sticking up for yourself? Look at the resistance in your body! Why is this stressing you out so badly? What are you so afraid of?"

I innately understood how my ego was holding me back from shining in all my glory, yet I meekly answered, "I don't know. I just feel that I should do the 'right' thing . . . that I'm being awful and unfair. Besides, doesn't our soul always want us to have peace?"

"What? Peace at the price of your personal integrity? I think not!" she practically screamed. "You're just letting yourself be bullied! It sounds to me like you're willing to forgo what's right—to avoid confrontation—just to ease your own guilt."

Wow . . . I'd never even considered that! But I also couldn't believe how much I was worrying about pleasing this certain person whom I barely knew, and who everyone else said was clearly taking advantage of me.

"Okay," Colette said, "tell me why you should forsake your own needs in order to make her [this particular woman whom I was so stressed out over] happy?"

The sleepless nights and pangs of anxiety were clear signs that something wasn't right, but I still didn't know how to deal with it and tell her that we weren't going to be working together. "I don't know why I can't stick up for myself and just tell her no," I replied in frustration. "I just keep hearing this little voice inside my head say, 'A good person would do the right thing and wouldn't put her own needs first. You're being selfish and greedy!'"

"That's ludicrous, Crystal," Colette retorted. "*I* won't let you be taken advantage of! And you're not being greedy—she is. Besides, who's the voice inside your head that keeps telling you this?"

"*Who* is the voice?" I repeated, surprised.

"Yes," she said. "Who is it?"

Completely dumbfounded, I answered, "It's me, I guess."

"No, it's not!" Colette exclaimed. "If it's *talking* to you, it's obviously *not* you . . . unless you have a multiple personality!" She laughed in her vivacious way.

I, somewhat confused and embarrassed, couldn't really understand where my friend was going. Yes, I grasped the whole concept of the ego and the soul, and I knew that my soul only wanted me to feel at peace, but Colette was venturing into a new territory I'd never thought about.

"Crystal, who is the voice inside your head?" she repeated. "What does it look like?" She waited, silently, and then added, "Close your eyes and tell me what it looks like."

Well, I must admit that I thought this was the most ridiculous thing I'd ever heard, but she insisted. "I can wait!" she said. "Tell me what this nasty little voice looks like."

For a long time, I couldn't come up with anything—and then, strangely enough, I began to see a tall, skinny, mean old nun with long gnarled fingers, standing over me, pointing and scowling down. (Don't ask me why I saw a nun—I'm not even Catholic.) "Shame on you," she was saying to me in my mind's eye, "shame on you for not being a good person!" And with that, I had a "face" for my voice.

Colette laughed again in her carefree but immensely loving way. "See!" she said. "And now when that old nun starts shaming you, you can talk back to her and let her know that she can just leave."

I can tell my nun to leave? Wow! This was one of the *biggest* "aha moments" of my life, as an incredible healing had just taken place. My nun was my ego, all the messages I'd heard my whole life, and I now had a face to this belittling and harsh voice inside of me.

I immediately felt a sense of awe, as well as a separation—and freedom—from my ego. I realized that the nun was merely a manifestation of the part of me that I'd been taught to fear, hide, and deny, and that her words were simply the negative messages that I heard when I was young. She was the personification of my fear of not being a "good little Christian girl," of not being nice enough . . . sweet enough . . . good enough.

I then began remembering how, when I was a little girl, my mother would tell me not to act like Nellie Oleson. (Do you remember the spoiled girl from *Little House on the Prairie*?) Being like Nellie was more than I could bear because I so wanted to be Laura Ingalls. I wanted it so desperately that I spent my life trying to please others, and whenever I acted in a way that was "Nellie-like," my old nun would start shaming me. The trouble remained because even though I was a grown woman, I was still trying to be like Laura Ingalls. Now, as noble and soulful as that sounds, I was a businessperson who often made choices that would hurt me rather than anyone else. I wasn't always speaking my truth or setting boundaries, and I clearly wasn't feeling empowered.

Once I realized that my nun wasn't actually me, I began talking back to her, telling her that I *was* a good person and that I needed to be good to me, too! I started telling her to go back to wherever she came from—I simply wasn't interested in hearing what she had to say anymore.

Each time I did this, I became stronger, realizing that I could silence this voice. I could be both gracious and strong, loving and firm, and fair and flexible. The trouble was that I could never get my nun to go away completely—she always seemed to pop up when I was under extreme stress. What was I doing wrong?

Then another lightbulb went off: I realized that as long as I saw my nun as my opponent, I'd always be at odds with myself. Since this mean old lady was *inside* and *a part* of me, as long as I resisted her, she'd persist. So I decided to look at her differently—

through the eyes of my soul. What a different image I saw! My nun was merely a frightened old woman who was terrified that we wouldn't be getting into heaven. She really believed that money was evil, that sex was only for procreation, and that having fun was the path paved to hell. She was taught to care what everyone else thinks and to be a martyr and a victim. She didn't know any better, and I knew that she only needed love and reassurance.

So now when my old nun starts belittling, judging, or trying to condemn me for anything—whether it's sipping a glass of wine, telling someone no, or making passionate love—I take her by the hand and sit her down in a rocking chair, put a blanket around her shoulders, and get her a cup of tea. "Everything will be okay," I'll tell her. "I'm just being me, and being me is perfectly okay."

Your ego might look like a mean old schoolteacher if being perceived as "disorganized, late, flighty, or absentminded" is be your worst fear. You may have a hairball (like one of my clients described her ego) that tells you that you're fat and ugly. Or you could have a dragon that breathes out fire and screams that you're a troublemaker and a loser. I once had a caller on my radio show tell me that her voice looked like a skunk and it kept telling her that she "stunk and was no good." So I asked her if she could picture that skunk as a terrified little animal who was just projecting *its* own fears onto her and was worried that the world would find out just how stinky it was. Her skunk was only trying to protect her.

The caller was really getting into the exercise and said with a laugh, "So I need to start loving my skunk, and maybe it will turn into Flower from *Bambi!*"

Exactly!

You see, once we view the scared or angry sides of us as petrified little animals caught in a trap, then we can learn to love *all of ourselves*. And once we do, our wild, untamed beasts become our domesticated, sweet pets.

The ego usually repeats the things we heard as children. So if we heard the messages (the injunctions) of, "Don't do that! Don't say that! Don't be that!" our ego took in those messages and continued to remind us of our "flaws" and how to cover them. Like a fierce mother bear, our ego thought that it was protecting us, but in the end it became our captor. And so we spend our lives trying hard to prove that we're okay. The trouble is that we get so caught up in the proving that we stop being. Feeling like a fraud, we're deathly afraid that the world will discover who we really are.

What's even worse is that we then begin attracting what we're emitting, and what we fear, we draw near. Just think of how many of us wake up 20, 30, or even 40 years later, and if we're absolutely honest with ourselves, have become the very thing we feared most. It's time to release our fears and focus on our strengths!

Would you like to try what my dear friend Colette did for me?

Close your eyes and picture your ego: What does it look like? Just say the very first thing that pops into your head and go with it. (If nothing comes, just wait—sometimes it takes a few minutes, but it will come. Don't resist this!) Is it dark? Is it big or small? Does it have a face? Is it a man or a woman, a monster, or a cartoon character? Is it fierce or terrified? Is it you at your worst? Can you draw a picture of your ego? Make it as real as you can.

One of my most fantastic clients, Katy, saw her ego simply as Thelma (yes, we named her), a nattering old nag who sported a ratty housecoat and curlers in her hair. Thelma kept telling Katy that she was never going to get married and that no one would ever love her if she acted like she was better than other people. Her ego did everything to keep Katy looking and acting like a wallflower, but Katy is now silencing Thelma. And when Thelma does start nagging and belittling, my client simply sees her as a worried old spinster who's afraid that life is going to pass her by. "It's okay, Thelma," Katy will reassure her. "I'm amazing. Don't worry—we're going to be okay!"

Once you learn to see your ego as separate and detached, and you embrace this voice—refusing to fight it—your ego will settle down and leave you alone. You'll see that taming the beast is better than fighting it. Remember, what you resist persists.

One of my beautiful clients, Wendy Fleet, wrote the following poem immediately after one of our coaching sessions. Wendy realized that she'd been hanging on and beating herself up for years over things that she couldn't change but couldn't let go of either. She wrote this piece in just five minutes, as her heart opened up and the words flowed out. She had no idea that she was a writer, but I felt such power in her words, and I think it pretty much sums up the hold our ego has over us if we let it.

Hello, demon . . . well, we meet again. You are here so often
that you feel like my second skin. I wonder sometimes
what it would be like to live a day without you in my life.
And then I remember why I have you here—to keep me safe
and stuck and living in my fear, but . . .
now something is going on . . . the tears are flowing strong.
It's like I'm waking up and the light is shining bright.
It is time to let you go . . . it will be hard, I know!
For I've had you here so long to remind me all that I've done wrong.
Living this way is not living at all. I know you're scared,
and so am I—without you I would not be where I am today.
I have to remember that, and all the mistakes that I've made.
The choices were, at the time, the best that I could do. So, demon,
I am saying good-bye to you—to fear and anger, judgment and shame.
To all the darkness in my heart that has caused me so much pain.

Remember that you're human—in all that it encompasses. Learn to love yourself, accept yourself, and set yourself free.

Become the "I Am"

One of the simplest secrets to surrendering and becoming the "I am" is to simply allow it to unfold within you. You don't ever need to worry or become frustrated when things don't seem to be going your way, because if it is meant to be, it will be. Once you've done all you can, release it, knowing that you never have to force anything or anyone.

Think about how many of us go against the very flow of life. We try so hard—pushing and pulling, arguing and stressing, worrying and resenting—without realizing that we're creating so much unnecessary turmoil and strife. We anticipate conversations, send angry e-mails, and choose to be "right" . . . only to find ourselves years later barely recognizing the person staring back at us in the mirror. We've spent our lives resisting the very essence of life—love, joy, peace, patience, integrity, and compassion. We neglect to discover that it's not about living on the "right" path, it's living on the path that's *right for us*.

When we worry, we reject the divinity of the Universe. We're essentially saying, "I know better than you do." But the soul never worries—it knows that the Universe will always provide, and that each experience is presented to us for a purpose: a specific learning lesson. It doesn't speculate about the future or dwell on the past. In fact, the soul never steps away from this moment into the distraction of the past or future. It can't and won't exist outside of this precise second because it understands with absolute certainty that "this" is all that's real—this second . . . now this second . . . wait, now it's this second. It never looks back and never looks forward, for both are an illusion. They don't exist.

The past and the future are false realities, and when we get stuck there—thinking, worrying, speculating, assuming, or fretting—we've let our mind-made self take over instead of abiding by our higher self. When we become acutely aware of our present moment and begin living in "the now" (the term Eckhart Tolle coined in his incredible book *The Power of Now*), we begin building trust in the flow of life again.

Most often, by just becoming "present" in all that you do—whether it's meditating or praying, washing the dishes, having a bath, or even driving in traffic—you'll discover the perfection in each moment. When you go outside, be highly aware of your surroundings: Feel the sun, hear the birds, and sniff the air, and don't let your mind wander off. When you're with family, laugh and cry with them, and leave knowing that you had a nice visit—don't overanalyze, assume, or look to be offended. When you're making love, be totally engaged and allow yourself to simply enjoy. As you read a book or listen to music, take pleasure in every word.

When you do catch yourself stepping out of the moment—moving into the past or future and letting your mind wander off—simply stop, become aware, and get engaged. It's in this awareness that you'll move back into the soul and reconnect with the joys in life. You'll laugh easier (because you'll take the time to really listen to a joke!), and you'll hug someone and actually feel their heart beating. You'll smell a rose, listen to waves crashing, pick up a paintbrush, write in a journal, go for a walk, or play with your children or grandchildren with ease and contentment. You'll cry, sing, dance, and feel. You'll live life! And it's here that you'll become the "I am" and feel most beautiful.

When you turn off the television, put down the fork, screw the top back on the bottle, and forget about who's done what and whom you're mad at, you'll begin to see the beauty that surrounds you. Your life will begin to unfold like a masterpiece, and you'll see all the living that needs to be done! You'll suddenly notice things that interest you: courses you want to take, people you'd like to meet, books you need to read, places you want to visit, and seeds you desire to plant in order for your life to bloom.

One of the biggest steps to transcending beauty is when we simply stop "trying" and "worrying" and start "being." A great actor, for example, doesn't try to play a role—instead, he becomes the role and it becomes him. The finest pianists don't try to play the piano—they let their soul create the music via their fingers. Or think about when you first fall in love: You don't try to be in love, you simply are. Fighting love is what causes us pain, not being in it.

When your baby is first born, you don't try to be a mother. And when you play a sport or do a hobby that you love—writing, painting, singing, running, yoga, whatever it may be—and you're totally engaged, you've stopped trying and you've become. Life becomes effortless, and everything falls perfectly into place.

When I'm writing and the words flow without thought or worry, I'm in the creation zone. But the minute I start getting frustrated and try to force sentences, I've stepped out of the soul and into my ego. My neck and upper back will start to throb, warning me that I'm no longer speaking my truth. If I continue this way, I'll be resisting what is as I try to make it what I want it to be.

Creation is a Divine process that simply works through you—you don't work it. When you're immersed in something and time stands still, you're in the soul. The brilliant humanistic psychologist Abraham Maslow eloquently shared that "what a man *can* be, he *must* be." In other words, you must align your energy with your highest potential, release your fears of the unknown, and share your God-given gifts with the world. We're waiting with excited anticipation . . . we need you!

When you focus 100 percent on being present, time becomes obsolete. You become aware of what *is*—not of what *was* or what *will be*. You don't worry about how you're going to handle the crisis brewing at work or if your relationship will last forever—you just know that all will work out as it should. You'll start trusting in others again, and even more important, you'll feel a sense of personal power that will allow you to release your need to be in control.

Every time you catch yourself worrying about your future or dwelling on your past—reliving arguments and letdowns—remind yourself that you've stepped out of the soul and into the ego. The most common word for the ego is *why?* But by focusing on the now and being acutely "present," you'll silence the beast and become.

Singing in the Rain

Not long ago, I did a weeklong workshop for women at a beautiful retreat in upstate New York. The surroundings were serene; the warm summer weather was perfect; and the food was all organic, unprocessed, and vegetarian. There were no telephones, televisions, radios, or computers. We all stayed in rustic cottages surrounded by 195 acres of rolling hills, plush gardens, and peaceful woodlands. Although the surroundings and lack of trappings were atypical for most of us, the women had traveled from all over North America to attend this powerful week of health and healing with me. And I was nervous and excited to be giving it.

As we sat gathered together on the first day, I looked around the room and saw women of all ages, races, and religions. I saw blondes, redheads, and brunettes . . . short and tall . . . thin and obese. There were quiet women, nervous women, outgoing women, and gentle women. There were professionals, stay-at-home moms, models, and corporate types. There were breathtakingly beautiful women and a few unsure, closed-off, angry ones. But what I saw (and felt) most were lonely women.

It wasn't because they lived alone or were personally "inept" in any way—rather, what I saw were women who *seemed to feel so alone* no matter how many people were around them. I instinctively knew that in *their* minds and hearts, they were too afraid to let anyone in.

One of the most simple, yet powerful, exercises that I did with these ladies during the week was to ask them to draw a picture of themselves in the rain. That was it—I gave them no other directions than that. The next day as we sat down in our circle, each person took a turn sharing her drawing and describing it. The first woman

(Continued on page 79 . . .)

Meditation

Meditation is an essential part of slowing your thoughts and becoming acutely present. During this intentional act of stillness, distractions may try to trickle in, and you may become aware of just how scattered and frightened your mind is—how much your ego is desperately trying to take over—yet it's in this "state of presence" that we're able to reconnect to the Divine Universal Collective Energy. Almost like plugging in to a rechargeable battery, it's here that we refuel. It's also here that we innately know that all will work out and that we're a part of a Divine blueprint—faith is embraced!

Meditation is sometimes defined as "listening to the silence between thoughts," for it's in stillness that the soul is revealed. This practice is also very useful for improving creativity and logic; enhancing mental clarity, reducing stress, and evoking clairvoyance; and balancing energy within the body. Many famous people such as Albert Einstein and Thomas Edison were known to have practiced various forms of meditation.

You want to keep your energy flow compact and intense, so your posture during meditation is important. The easiest position is sitting comfortably, with your hands joined and your legs crossed. Sitting cross-legged is another good option, but it requires some fitness and training. If you lie down, you may fall asleep, so try to practice sitting up.

If you've never meditated before, find a quiet spot. Don't get too worried about chanting mantras (a repeated phrase), although it does help to keep the mind from becoming distracted, as does focusing on a lit candle or a beautiful flower. Five minutes of meditating to begin with is excellent, and over time you may want to try to build up to 20- or 30-minute sessions.

Try the following steps to get started:

1. Adopt a comfortable meditation posture as outlined above.

2. Close your eyes and take some deep breaths through your nose. Inhale at the same speed as you exhale. It makes no difference if you inhale for a beat of three and then exhale for a beat of three or use a beat of five—it all depends on your own lung capacity and what feels best for you. You can also try breathing in through only one nostril by closing one with your finger while you inhale, and then switch while you exhale. Take deep breaths and visualize inhaling pure, cleansing air.

3. Next, focus on relaxing all the muscles in your body, beginning at your toes and working all the way to the top of your head, including your face. (If this is difficult for you, please try my *Relaxation Therapy* CD available at **www.crystalandrus.com.**)

4. Once you feel totally relaxed, visualize a white healing light in your mind's eye, flowing freely from the top of your head down to your feet and back up again, paying special attention to any area that you may be having pain in. Hold your hand above the area and focus on visualizing the white light flowing freely throughout your body.

5. Once your body is in a deep state of relaxation, focus on eliminating all thoughts as

they enter your mind. You can use a mental sound, such as "Ooooohhmmm" (a mantra), every time you have a thought, or try saying something powerful such as: "I will still my mind to connect to the Divine."

6. Once you can get down to two or three thoughts in five minutes, you've meditated successfully! Know that each day it will get easier and more intensely healing.

Even just ten minutes of meditation a day can evoke a calm and connectedness, so make this a part of your daily practice.

drew a picture of herself dancing in the rain, smiling and free. But then directly next to it, there was a second picture where she was bent over, hands over her head, face tucked into her chest, running from the rain. As she began to explain it, she unexpectedly burst into tears.

"This is how I want to be," she cried, as she pointed to the first fearless woman. "But I immediately realized that I'd never dance free in the rain. I'd hide and run, cover up, afraid to just *be*. . . ."

We continued on. The next woman had drawn herself in color, wearing a bright red raincoat. Her hair was styled perfectly, even though it was raining quite hard in her picture. She had no umbrella, no galoshes, and no rain hat on. But something struck me: She'd drawn herself from behind. She had no face—just a red raincoat and perfect blonde hair. Her back was turned to the world . . . and on herself.

Around the circle we went. Most had drawn pictures of themselves under huge umbrellas, wearing rain boots, raincoats, and hats. Some drew lightning flashing across the sky. Others penciled in dark clouds and very heavy rain falling around them. A few put rainbows and flowers on their picture; and one woman drew herself running along a tree-lined path with a friend. And then we got to an absolutely beautiful woman—on the inside and out—who was a naturopathic doctor and psychologist. As she held up her picture, everyone smiled. There she was, dancing with her arms lifted to the sky, engulfed in heart-shaped raindrops. "I am love. I know the Universe is filled with love, and I am open to receiving it," she eloquently shared.

Most were beginning to "get" what this exercise represented . . . and then we got to the quietest (and largest) woman in the room. She'd been struggling during the week, didn't open up much during any of the group-sharing sessions, and would always disappear just as we were getting started with our workout each day. She'd tried every diet known to man and had even had gastric bypass surgery. She was on special herbs and receiving acupuncture . . . and she was tired, fed up, frustrated, closed down, discontent, and absolutely disheartened. She was at least 350 pounds, and had talked with me privately about how she didn't want anyone to tell her what to do—not here or anywhere else in her life. I think that she really thought this was going to be one more stupid "fat camp" and that at the end of the week she could at least say to herself (or maybe to her family): "I've tried everything. It's not my fault."

As she proudly showed her picture off that morning, lightbulbs went off over everyone's heads. There she was, a tiny stick figure hiding inside a huge brick house, with torrential rain pouring down and fierce lightning crackling around her home. You could barely even see her through the window. She smiled as she proudly declared how smart she felt to have drawn herself this way—how protected she was, and how nothing could hurt her. No rain was ever going to get *her* wet!

The Seat of the Soul and the Essence of Beauty

When trust in the world or other people is missing, we stop abiding by our higher self. We stop being honest, and we give away our power. And we see an unattractive person when we look into the mirror, fearful that the world may see her, too.

This is not a consciously deceitful act, but an individual who lacks trust stops trusting in herself. She disconnects, unknowingly lets her mind-made self take over, and begins resisting the flow of life. Unaware, she dims her own light. And no matter how openly she may smile or how much fun she might appear to be, she never feels truly secure, content, and at ease.

The trust I'm talking about is the childlike sense that's derived from an inherent feeling of safety. If a person doubts the world—doubts love, safety, comfort, security, and abundance—then she'll ultimately doubt herself and will end up sabotaging everything from relationships and jobs to her health and well-being. Afraid to trust in the Universe, she'll need to stay in control of everything, and when she feels as if she's losing control, anxiety, insecurity, worry, anger, self-righteousness, defensiveness, fear, indifference, aloofness, aggression, denial, and even distraction will takes over.

Distraction is one of the sneakiest saboteurs of the ego because most often we don't even know that we're distracted. Since the ego relies purely on problem solving (the "logical mind"), it thrives on crisis and will actually search out problems just to make it feel important when it can solve them. We stay so busy *being* busy that we're just too busy to notice! So we often forget that the soul is detached from outcome and expectation, and that living with simplicity and passion should feel effortless.

As Keith Sherwood, author of *Chakra Therapy,* explains:

> A person who lacks trust will be prevented from achieving his personal goal of wholeness and unconditional joy. Moreover, a person who lacks trust must continuously block the feelings of emptiness and despair imprisoned within him from rising to the surface. . . . Self indulgence is the alternative chosen . . . it takes the form of all sorts of addictive behavior, from overeating to excessive worrying, self-importance, arrogance to depression, alcoholism and even drug addiction and suicide. You indulge yourself when you are not being yourself. . . .

Most of us aren't aware of how deep our inability to trust directs our lives, or even that we *are* distrustful. But our soul will show us our fears through our bodies and our emotions. Those who suffer with eating disorders or obesity; addictions; indigestion, ulcers, hernias, irritable bowel syndrome, constipation, or abdominal afflictions; problems with the liver, gallbladder, pancreas, adrenal glands, spleen, or kidney; and weight gain around the middle often struggle with trust issues. Endometriosis, PMS, infertility, bladder infections, uterine or ovarian pain, and even middle- and lower-back trouble are all signs that we may be carrying blocked emotional energy, which stems from an inability to trust. This is about control, and when we must control what is, we can never shine . . . or transcend.

Because of this deep fear, we suffer from low self-esteem and a lack of confidence and self-respect, and we have a difficult time committing to others. It's too hard to put our faith in someone else when we don't even trust ourselves. We often find ourselves overly sensitive, wondering why people are so dishonest, and we feel confused about what our passion is. We test friends and lovers, pushing them away and seeing if they'll come back for more. The control gives us temporary power, but it inevitably ends up robbing us of our own light. Soon we find that we've stopped listening to our gut and instead numbed it with whatever learned coping mechanism we've adopted (often eating or drinking). And this is the perfect breeding ground for the ego.

Trust is the seat of the soul and the essence of beauty. Trust is letting go and letting God. And ironically enough, it's often our resistance that keeps us from releasing it. "No, I don't have any trust problems—I'm just being careful and wise," we insist, as we hold on tighter, claiming that we have no control issues!

Getting back to the women who'd embarked on this retreat with me in New York, the experience was quite remarkable for them. Bless their souls, they thought that they'd signed up for a "boot camp" to get them into great physical shape. Happily, though, they each left realizing that weight is only a manifestation of something so much deeper. And although most of them departed at least five pounds lighter, what I mainly noticed was that they suddenly had a bounce in their step and a twinkle in their eyes.

That picture in the rain represents our sense of personal power in the world and our ability to trust in ourselves—to live fearlessly and know that we, alone, are enough, *without our masks.* The rain and sky symbolize how we perceive our life challenges; and umbrellas, hats, and boots (or a lack thereof) are our need to protect ourselves from the world. Everything from what we're wearing to how big or small we appear on the page to if we're turning our back on ourselves or raising our hands to the sky can be clues to how much trust and personal power we feel.

But trust and power, just like a muscle, can always be built back up. No matter what you've gone through in your life—and no matter how painful it was—you can make the choice to align your personality with your soul and *become.* You can surrender and let the Universe shower its love upon you!

It begins by taming the beast, for once you begin to silence it, you'll begin to hear your true voice . . . that of your higher self. It's then that you must believe and truly trust in yourself, for when you do, you'll be able to start opening up and letting others see you for who you really are. By speaking *your* truth, you'll begin to set yourself free. This takes courage. By this, I don't mean the heroism that we see in a crisis—it's the courage to give nobility to your life, to choose to be yourself above what other people want you to be, and to take the path that's right for you . . . the path of least resistance! Let down your walls and embrace the world, which is filled with so many wonderful and amazing people who only want to love and trust, too. Always remember that your outer world is just a reflection of your inner world—it will only change when you change.

Our woman "hiding in the house" stood up on the last day and told us, "I feel like I've spent my life searching for the answers as to why I was the fat one. Why had this happened to me? Who was going to fix me? And when was it going to happen? And then I realized over this past week that maybe it's the searching that has stopped me from finding. That maybe, just like in *The Wizard of Oz,* I'm Dorothy and I've always had the power . . . I just never knew it until now."

I smiled wide because she'd gotten it! And as we began to cheer for her, the rain started to pour down outside. (Believe it or not!) After we said our good-byes, many of the women unconsciously popped open their umbrellas on their way out the door. But as I looked out the window and saw them making their way down the long dirt path toward their cars, I watched in amazement as most of the umbrellas came down, one by one. These honest, beautiful, fearless women were walking tall, strong, and carefree . . . *singing in the rain.* They realized that they have all the power they'll ever need, nestled deep within.

All *you* have to do is believe it—the rest will take care of itself! It's so much simpler than you realize.

Searching is often the devious distraction from ever attaining.
You have all the answers within you . . . know it!

To be or not to be:
That is the question.
— William Shakespeare

Chapter Four

The Body Has a "Knowingness"

You wake up to the sound of a blaring alarm clock and immediately think, *Oh, God, it's morning already?*

Jumping up, you rush into your bathroom, tripping over your husband's pile of dirty laundry lying on the floor. *I'm sick of his mess, and I hate this tiny bathroom.*

Still half asleep, you get in the shower and scrape a dull razor over your legs, nicking yourself in the process. *Damn it!* Climbing out onto the cold floor, you curse the winter: *I can't stand this weather much longer—I hate where we live!*

Wiping the foggy mirror, you stare, shocked at the face looking back at you. *Oh my, I need some serious work today.* Opening up the bathroom drawer that's filled with 18 tubes of red lipstick, you fish out your most recent buy, Remarkable Red. *Nothing remarkable about this mouth* flashes through your mind as you smudge it over your lips.

Scanning the floor of your closet for your baggy pants and oversized sweater, you notice a pair of knee-high boots. *Did I actually wear those once? What was I thinking?*

You walk into your kitchen and swing open the refrigerator door. A few bottles of pickles, some hot sauce, three doughnuts, and four eggs (that you can't remember buying) look back at you. You opt for one of the stale doughnuts as you grab your cigarettes and scurry out the door late for work. *I'm so tired. I guess I'll grab some coffee on the way. Another week begins. . . .*

Too many people live on an emotional daily roller coaster. Over the course of the day, they go from up to down, happy to sad, and motivated to depressed—all within a matter of hours—completely unaware that every choice they make creates their life. It's natural and normal to sporadically have quiet, or even low, moments, as this is often an indication that a "ladder" is coming. However, living with constant surges of happiness followed by indifference or despair is *not* natural (although it has become normal in our culture).

Your beauty, or your light, comes from the choices you make each day. Your life is a culmination of the regular days, not the momentous ones that stand out over time, so how have you spent yours? How have you celebrated *you?* What did you see when you looked in the mirror?

Let's compare the difference between the previous "morning scene" with another. . . .

You wake up to the sound of soft music and think, *Ah, 5:30 A.M. It's so great that I have two hours before I have to leave for work.* You roll over and kiss your husband softly on his back.

Quietly tiptoeing down your dark hallway to your cozy kitchen, you light a candle and put on the kettle for a cup of hot lemon tea. *I love this time alone.*

Sipping on your brew, you saunter into your magical little living room and slide on your running shoes. As you hit the fresh morning air, you take a deep breath and thank God for your healthy body. You begin to move in rhythm with your beating heart as you listen to the birds sing. *I feel so strong today!*

Forty minutes later, you climb into your hot bubble bath and light some candles around the edge. With care and ease, you slide the razor over your legs, feeling the moisture of the bath oils. After ten relaxing and rejuvenating minutes, you step from your small but peaceful sanctuary and peer into the mirror. *Not bad for two kids!* And as you carefully polish your lips with gloss, you honor your reflection by smiling back. *I could be better . . . I could be worse . . . but I'm happy right where I am.*

Opening your closet, you effortlessly pull on your favorite dress. *I love the way this gently hugs my curves!* And just as you're about to leave, your husband comes around the corner with a protein shake, your vitamins, and your lunch. Your final thought out the door is: *It's going to be a great day.*

Your life . . . your choices!

Mirror, Mirror on the Wall

I'd be lying if I said that I've never looked in the mirror and wished for something different. But I've also learned over the years that when I don't focus so much on my refelection, I forget about my so-called flaws. I wonder why so many of us spend so much time wishing that things were different and believing that changes would finally make us happy.

Here's something to try: Stop looking at yourself so much! As silly as that sounds, it's often those of us who are fixated on our reflections who have the hardest time accepting what we see with ease and contentment. When we're constantly focusing on our flaws, we end up completely overlooking our perfection. Besides, our bodies truly have a "knowingness," right down to the cellular level, of when we're in sync, connected, and at peace. And since we'll turn into whatever we focus on, we can't become healthy, vital, beautiful, and content unless we feel it!

So how about taking that mirror sabbatical, for even just a week? Get ready in the morning using it as little as possible, and try to avoid it during the day. No more deep analyzing of your pores and wrinkles, the back of your hair, or your full-length profile—just give yourself a break.

While you're at it, why not cease watching television shows that distort your perception of reality—your notion of what's normal, healthy, and beautiful? To that end, you could also stop buying beauty and fitness magazines that play off of your insecurities with the promise that something within their pages will "fix" you. *You're not broken!* There's nothing inside any magazine that will give you the answers you're looking for.

Sadly, so many of us have given away our own power by allowing the cosmetics, fashion, diet, and entertainment industries to make a trade out of our fears. They tell us whatever they think we want to hear, and we listen, nodding our heads, while holding our hands out for more.

Stop! Understand that these entities are simply about making money, nothing more. It's supply and demand: If we didn't buy it, they wouldn't provide it. And as long as they get their ratings or sell their products, they'll keep on delivering.

We buy fashion magazines because we want to believe that if we follow their advice—with enough makeup, styling, wrinkle creams, dieting, and designer outfits—we may be able to look like the models who adorn the covers. Having said that, I'm certainly not diminishing these genetically gifted beauties. Models are simply the messengers—it's the advertisers who manipulate us with false promises, misleading pictures, and the notion that with enough work we can feel good.

But what if we discovered that our own beauty is already within us and that, if given the nurturing and love we need, each one of us can blossom into a gorgeous rose . . . or perhaps a daffodil . . . or maybe a tropical orchid! (Imagine if only the rose was considered beautiful?)

Until we redefine our concept of what "beautiful" is, we're going to stay captive to our mind-made version. Yet once we claim our own beauty and stop buying into the myth that we have to be something different from what we are, we'll force advertisers, editors, producers, and directors to market their products differently—with intelligence and respect. The economy will still survive!

What's most important for us to realize is that we women are not competitors—in other words, just as no one's intelligence can take away from yours, no other woman's beauty can take away from yours either. For just as nature is perfect and lovingly accepts itself, we, too, must accept ourselves. The bird doesn't look enviously at the butterfly, the birch tree doesn't ache to be an oak, and the ocean doesn't ask to be the stars. Rather, each knows that it's created in perfect harmony, connected to the other, and that its own strength and vitality depends upon each other.

We're all just as connected as nature is—we all come from the same sea of Divine universal love—and until we realize that your success is my success and vice versa, we'll never be truly powerful. Understand that I am you and you are me. Simply put: Our strength and power lie in our appreciation of each other. So start looking around at the real world with loving, compassionate eyes. Notice other women, and search for the beauty in each one. Once you can see that there's no *one* ideal but rather *all* ideals, then you'll innately know that there are no mistakes—each person was created in the Divine likeness of perfection. And you are perfect, too.

I tell a funny little story in my first book, *Simply . . . Woman!* After losing a lot of weight, I planned a trip to the beach with my family. While we were getting organized for the outing, my mind was racing—I imagined gorgeous, firm little bodies in string bikinis all over the sand. But the reality could not have been further from the truth. Sure, there were the typically perky 20-year-olds, but I saw normal women, too . . . most with cellulite and rounded hips; and many sporting stretch marks, loose skin, and sagging breasts.

The girls of *Baywatch* aren't on our beaches, and I'd been comparing myself with ridiculous ideals. It was time that I accepted myself for me—but just as important, it was time that I honored all other women for their authentic beauty, too. The thin and heavy ones . . . the shapely and athletic . . . the tall and short. Once I began seeing past the exteriors of other women, it became so easy to see the light that shone within each one. Some were brighter, some were dimmer, and quite ironically, the brightest lights were often in the simplest packages.

As time went by and I just observed people, I began to notice how sad and uncertain so many stereotypically "beautiful" women seemed. I'd watch as many walked by with "an air" that seemed put on, and I'd notice as they'd scan windows for their reflections, worried if a hair was out of place or their lipstick had rubbed off. I intuitively knew that for so much of their lives, they'd depended upon their looks for attention and approval, not considering that they could never hear "You're beautiful" enough to innately know it from within. I knew this with such certainty because it had once been me, too.

A huge part of making peace with yourself and seeing the beauty you already possess comes from letting go of your idea of what you're supposed to be. It's your ego that points out other women and tries to convince you that you're less than they are, that your butt is too big or your breasts are too small. And as long as you're listening to this "I" of the mind, you're going to have frustrations, fears, pain, expectations, and attachments to outcomes.

Being confident and learning to really love yourself and your reflection can take some effort because you really only have three choices: change it, release it, or continue to suffer. As David Simon, M.D., the author of *Vital Energy,* says, "Once you make your choices conscious, it is much more difficult to choose to suffer." You can't change who you are, but you *can* release your resistance and redefine your beliefs.

This reminds me of my youngest daughter, who used to cry and complain about her gorgeous, thick, curly hair, wishing that it were thin, straight, and "not so puffy." As she'd slick it back tight into a bun every day for school, I'd tell her, "Imagine a beautiful place in nature in which you'd want to build your home: You could go into the natural surroundings and work with the exquisiteness, tenderly and lovingly using what you've been given to create a masterpiece, or you could go in and clear-cut the forest because you want to re-create beauty based on your ego's version of what beautiful is.

"Sweetheart," I'd firmly but lovingly tell her, "*you* are that raw piece of nature, and once you see the beauty you already possess, then you'll begin to lovingly work with what God has given you! Sure, use hair products that will eliminate frizz, and let's get a great cut, but you can't shave your head or change the hair you have, so crying about it every day and wishing that you could is pointless and self-defeating. Love and honor the hair you have, and I promise you that it will begin to love and honor you back."

Does this sound familiar to you? Maybe when you look in the mirror, you wish that your eyes were a different color, your nose was smaller, or your lips were bigger. Perhaps you cry for longer legs, fuller breasts, or a tinier waist. But the damn-straight truth is that you have to work with what God has given you, and you *must* learn to *see* beauty in order to *be* beauty . . . and for anyone else to see it, too!

Remember that your mind isn't just housed in that organ of yours called a brain—it's in each one of your hundred trillion cells, talking to them with every thought you think and every word you speak. When you love and honor your body, it will love and honor you back. When you thank your legs for carrying you around through this lifetime, they will thank you in return. When you thank your eyes for showing you such beauty and your nose for giving you such wondrous scents, they'll rejoice in your gratitude. When you thank your arms for the love they've embraced, they feel it and will embrace you back. *The body has a knowingness!*

What's most amazing about all this for me is that once I stopped scrubbing my skin, squeezing my pores, examining my lines, and layering my face with thick foundation and powder every day—desperately trying to cover up my imperfections—and just declared out loud, "You are what you are," my skin began to rejoice in its freedom and started to glow as though I were in love. And I guess I *was* in love . . . with me!

I truly don't know if it was that my skin could finally breathe or that my epidermis's cells finally knew that they were loved and began loving me back, but my breakouts diminished and my "flaws" seemed to be far less noticeable (or perhaps my reality simply aligned to my new perceptions).

This is very similar to what happened to one of the wonderful women on my Website's message forum, who shared this post regarding her breasts: "I remember being about 16 and feeling *so* embarrassed because I only had an A-cup bra. Actually not just embarrassed, but ashamed. Now that I've begun to really value my body and embrace my body as sacred (which it is), I swear that my boobs have gotten nicer! I'm sure that they were beautiful all along, but now I know it."

The Mirror Exercise

Take some time on a quiet morning (or whenever you're ready to finally make peace with your reflection), get out a handheld mirror, and look at yourself without any makeup. Take a few minutes to gaze at your face, looking deeply at your eyes, nose, cheeks, lips, teeth, and forehead. What do think? What beliefs have you developed? Do you see beautiful eyes? Do you like the color and shape of them, or do you wish that you could change them? How about your nose—is it striking and unique or ugly and protruding? What about your lips, teeth, skin, chin, cheekbones, and ears? Are you happy with your reflection?

Now, look at your face as a whole. Move back from the mirror and tilt your head from side to side and smile. Really smile. Notice how your eyes curl up and the apples of your cheeks rise . . . aren't you lovely?

A way to help you make peace with your own reflection is to list all of the imperfections you see on your face and body (without clothes or makeup) in your journal. Then beside each supposed flaw, note where or who you think that belief originated from. For example, if you see yourself with a nose too big or legs too short, who told you that? (You can actually do this with any area of your life that you're struggling with, from your sexuality and finances to your eating and exercise habits.)

You'll soon see that almost all the negative thoughts you have about yourself came from someone else's belief systems, whether it was a member of your family, a friend, a mate, or the media. And as long as you continue to believe these messages, you're powerless to change them.

Look over these beliefs, and answer the following questions in your journal:

- Are these beliefs serving you now?

- If not, how have you held yourself back by believing them? What have you lost out on in life because of these beliefs?

- What have you gained by believing them? In other words, how have you let them become your excuse for not demanding more for your life?

- Can you let go of your negative beliefs about your looks? Do you want to?

- When?

Once you've decided that you're ready to let go of these old self-defeating beliefs, realizing that they no longer own you, tear the list out of your journal and burn it. Yes, you heard me right. Don't just crumple it up and toss it into the garbage—it must be burned. You can use a fireplace, a barbeque, or do it outside in a large tin pan. Once that list is merely ashes, blow it away into the wind. These messages are now gone—they're longer serving you, so you must not own them anymore.

The Top 15 Ways to Dramatically Increase Energy

1. Smile!
2. Listen to music that stirs your soul.
3. Get some fresh air.
4. Turn off the TV and read a good book.
5. Move your body—dance, run, stretch, or skip.
6. Help someone . . . expecting nothing in return.
7. Eat rich bioenergetic foods.
8. Be acutely aware of staying in the moment.
9. Make passionate love!
10. Pray or meditate.
11. Drink plenty of water and take high-quality nutritional supplements daily.
12. Live with purpose—follow your heart's desires!
13. Keep your house and work space clean and clutter free.
14. Light candles and dim the lamps.
15. Tell someone you love them and hug them tight!

Next, imagine that the person writing these beliefs is your higher self. Begin to make a new list in your journal. This time, jot down all the things that you originally listed that you didn't like, but now find something about that feature or body part that you *do* like. If you're finding it difficult, imagine that you're describing your child, best friend, or favorite actress—no matter how long it takes, you must write something positive about every part of you.

After you've rewritten your supposed flaws as perfections, note all the other things that you really *do* like about yourself—the more, the better! Search for every small detail, and continue with this exercise until you're able to create a list of things that celebrate the beauty and passion that you possess. *This list is the real you.*

It's so important that you become comfortable with yourself, with and without clothes and makeup, and that you verbally proclaim your beauty every day. Read your new list daily while facing the mirror. It may take a little while until you finally begin to embrace your beauty and make peace with yourself, and that's okay.

It will still begin to manifest into your thoughts and into every single one of your 100 trillion cells. Fake it till you make it!

Read your list with passion, and look in the mirror and *smile.* And on the days when you can't help but notice your flaws, stop looking. Quit picking and pointing out the things you wished you could change—remember, you have to first *see* beautiful to *be* beautiful!

One day you'll find yourself happily aware that you're no longer putting yourself down and bringing constant attention to your supposed flaws. You'll also become pleasantly surprised when, before you know it, you're no longer faking it . . . you *are* it.

The Colors of the Rainbow

For most of my life, food was the enemy. Whether I was mad at myself for what I ate or obsessively counting calories to know if I *could* eat, I was a prisoner to food. It either comforted or hurt me: I'd either be "good," eating really strict and controlled portions, or "bad," eating everything and anything. I was totally black or white.

The truth is that I was pretty much that way when it came to everything in my life. No one else ever needed to get mad at me for the things I said or did (or didn't say or do) because I was the best punisher ever. I'd beat myself up if I messed up at work or said something without thinking first. I'd bury myself in my own private cell if I had thoughts that didn't seem "Christian" or if I acted "inappropriately."

Sad, I think, as I look back now. Yet I also joyously sigh with relief that I escaped that mind-made prison of black and white. What freedom it is to live with all the colors of the rainbow!

Food, just like drugs or alcohol, can temporarily numb us, but unlike those others, the simple fact is that we can't run from food because we need it to live. Food is not the enemy! Do you understand that eating—just like drinking, making love, dancing, praying, meditating, and laughing—isn't "good" or "bad," it just *is?* It's merely one part of our lives, and it shouldn't take over our existence or dictate our emotions. Most of us have been programmed to think of food as either "guilt free" or "guilt ridden," but this mind-set is in its very essence fundamentally flawed. Instead, we should simply think of food as energy, without attachment to the labels we've created.

Not long ago, I did a TV show with a woman from Overeaters Anonymous (OA), and I felt so sad for her. She sat on the set in full disguise, weighing at least 300 pounds, claiming that at OA she could be herself, among like-minded people who understood her "disease." She declared on the air that she was powerless when it came to food and that telling her to "just stop eating" and push herself away from the table would never work.

I wanted to take this woman by the hands, look in her eyes, and tell her that this was about something so much deeper than broccoli or cookies. She wasn't powerless, but her ego was, and as long as she allowed it to drive her life, she'd continue to feel out of control. She'd merely lost her voice—her personal power, integrity, and innate sense of wonder and beauty—and somewhere along the way had resigned herself to believing that being morbidly obese and miserable was her destiny.

I don't believe this is true, not for anyone. I know, for I once felt powerless, too. You see, at age 18, I moved in with my bodybuilder boyfriend (soon to be my husband). He worked at my mom's gym, and I found myself falling right into their world—the one I'd rejected for as long as I could remember—the world of bodybuilding.

As soon as I began training with weights, my body responded as though I were made for it. Because my mother was so well known in the industry (she was a national-level competitive bodybuilder), I was immediately approached by a television station to do a show called *Really Me on YTV.* The producer told me that I was meant for the screen, and as he stroked my soul and nourished my growing ego, I decided that maybe I'd follow in my mother's footsteps and try out the stage, too.

Three months later, I competed in, and won, my first provincial-level bodybuilding show. Winning seemed to be almost effortless for me, yet the experience left me feeling empty—not like a winner at all. I hated looking at the pictures afterward because I didn't have half the body my mother did (at least that's how I felt). That would be the end of that!

I decided that since bodybuilding wasn't for me, maybe modeling would make me happier. Everyone always said I had a pretty face, and it felt like a less obtrusive and exploitive industry. I worked hard at making myself perfect, yet when I looked in the mirror, all I saw were things I had to change. Insecurities drove me . . . and drove me crazy. No matter how good I looked, it was never good enough. Sadly, I had become a swan who still felt like the ugly duckling.

It didn't help that my boyfriend was even more consumed than I (but with his own body), and that together our lives were entirely driven by our looks. Yet I felt the constant aching inside. To me, beauty and brawn were the enemies—why didn't anyone else in my world see how stressed we all were trying to look flawless?

By the time I was 22, I was married, running a chain of fitness clubs, and had just opened Crystal's Health and Fitness Spa. I had nearly 100 employees who answered to me, I'd bought my first home, and I had money in the bank. It seemed that I was powerful, and I was sure that I'd feel successful soon. Still, my emptiness prevailed.

So I went back to try my hand at "fitness shows." After being invited to compete against 250 women at my first international competition, Ms. Galaxy, I decided I was going to prove that I was somebody important. I spent a week with judges, competitors, and photographers, oiled up and strutting my stuff each day. The first round put me in seventh place, yet I'd go to sleep each night dreading the next day, wishing for the week to be over. How interesting that on the fourth day I sprained my ankle and tore all the ligaments in my right shoulder! I returned home on crutches, feeling even more defeated. However, the photos had been taken, and months later I was popping up in magazines all over North America. But that came a little too late . . . because I was already pregnant.

The minute I got home, I'd decided to pack it all in. Believing that babies would fulfill me and that a white picket fence would give me the happiness I was searching for, I focused 100 percent on being the perfect mom and wife. I moved my family out of the city and to a gorgeous house in a picturesque small town. I cooked gourmet meals, made bread from scratch, and scrubbed my newly renovated home from top to bottom. Soon cooking, decorating, cleaning, and changing diapers became my distractions of choice. I was a perfectionist, and I did everything with fierce determination. I also began eating like never before.

Having gained 80 pounds during my first pregnancy, which I didn't completely lose before going through my second, I felt crippled with self-loathing and disgust. Photographers were calling, and companies looking for spokespeople were knocking on my door . . . but I certainly didn't answer. I was fat now—imagine what they'd think!

Instead, I hibernated in my house and convinced myself that my dreams were vain, shallow, and totally self-serving. Besides, I had so many things to be grateful for. Still, all I could focus on was my weight. I'd spent over three years being pregnant and nursing that I didn't even know who I was anymore. But had I ever, really?

Thankfully, when my second daughter was about four months old, I had an aha moment that changed the course of my life. As I sat in my rocking chair and nursed her, I sobbed as I realized that I was cheating both my girls of the most important lesson in life: self-love. And in that moment, I became utterly and profoundly aware that I was solely and exclusively accountable for my life—my thoughts, words, and actions—and that my unhappiness wasn't just about my weight, even though that's what I was entirely focused on.

I realized that I'd been hurting since my parents' divorce when I was 12 years old (and angry since my rape at 14), but I'd never faced it. It wasn't really about cookies and chocolate or fitness shows and photo shoots—my pain had simply manifested in different ways. And on that very day, nearly ten years ago, I began a life-changing journey in which I not only lost all my extra fat, but I also began to shed my emotional baggage. I started listening to my gut instead of feeding it! It was scary at times, but the alternative was even scarier.

I went out the next morning and started walking, and those walks turned into jogs, and the jogs turned into strength. A power was building in me that I never knew I had. I also started eating more healthfully and pouring my heart and soul out into my journals. I had such breakthroughs and revelations that to this day, I still don't know how the lights turned on so brightly. Sometimes they woke me from deep sleep, while at other times, they came when I was out on a long run. Things started to become clearer. The fog was lifting, my anger was dissipating, and love started rushing through my veins. Everything started to make sense to me, and I began to accept that everything I'd ever been through had just been preparation for the life I was intended to live . . . the words I was meant to write . . . the gift I was meant to share.

The first step to taking back your body and/or health is to redefine your association to food, exercise, and beauty by affirming new thought patterns about them.

One of the main things that personal trainers and coaches do is create a goal-setting system and exercise routine that not only empowers their clients to achieve their specific goals, but also makes those goals measurable, attainable, and realistic. Yet the trouble with this is that in a world where less than 2 percent of women feel beautiful, and where we're led to believe that beauty only comes if we're 5' 11" and 110 pounds, achieving "realistic and attainable" goals is simply *not* realistic or attainable. So most of us end up setting ourselves up for disappointment, without ever realizing that it was our belief of what we "should be" that created this almost-guaranteed recipe for failure. In other words, as long as we hold on to our idea of what's "ideal," then no matter how much work we do, we'll always be attached to a preconceived (and most often totally unrealistic) notion of it. Thus, no matter how successful we are, it will never be enough . . . and in our frustration, we end up giving up completely.

Why not turn things around by first redefining your concept of what "fit," "successful," and "beautiful" are? This way, attaining them (in your mind at least) will be *possible.* Try creating a whole new belief structure that truly is about health, strength, and self-empowerment, and then come up with some success markers that celebrate your achievements rather than beating yourself up if you fall behind.

Next, accept that food is a fuel source, and punishing yourself because you ate something that you thought you shouldn't have shifts your resonance to that of shame, regret, and guilt. Food and drink are not evil, and eating and drinking shouldn't feel shameful or embarrassing. Food is a life-giving celebration, and enjoying a meal is the only way to eat.

I recently watched an interview with Mireille Guiliano, the author of *French Women Don't Get Fat,* and I listened with surprised joy as she said what I felt. Ms. Guiliano spoke of how we should all eat and celebrate life without self-loathing or punishment, so if we crave a little something sweet, it's not the end of the world. We should have it—and *enjoy* it. (But we need to remember portion control and to nourish ourselves with plenty of healthy food, too.)

The second step is to realize that different foods have different "octane" or energy levels. Since energy is never lost, it's only transferred, everything you eat affects your energy level. So dining on a large salad, some organic fruit, and some fresh fish will make you feel alive and energized, while downing a burger and fries will make you tired and sluggish.

To understand the difference between rich bioenergetic foods versus low-calibrating substances, compare it to how your car runs when you put in high-octane gas compared with low-octane fuel. All gasoline, no matter what the octane level, has the same amount of "calories" per gallon, just as all carbohydrates—regardless of if they're refined and processed or whole grain and natural—all contain four calories per gram. The difference between high-octane and low-octane fuels is that once in your vehicle's engine, the high-octane stuff allows the extraction of more of the potential energy because the quality of the fuel allows your car to perform better. Following the same principle, high-octane foods allow your body to perform better. You'll become more powerful, more energized, healthier, slimmer, and disease free.

There are rich bioenergetic foods that when digested transfer into our body as abundant, easily accessible energy, and when we eat them, our cells rejoice. Conversely, when we eat foods that are low in octane, our cells become starved for vitamins, minerals, essential fatty acids, bioflavonoids, digestive enzymes, antioxidants, fiber, phyto (plant) nutrients, and essential amino acids, and in their "starvation mode," they begin to slow down. Obesity, depression, illness, disease, and fatigue then take over.

Our bodies were designed to be energy-creating machines. When we eat high-octane foods, our cells actually begin to move quicker: Our metabolism speeds up, we burn body fat easily, and we have an abundance of energy—thin thighs are just a byproduct of healthy eating!

Saying Grace

When we give thanks for our food and ask the Divine to bless it in our bodies, we send our cells the powerful messages that we know they'll "do right" by our food and that the nutrients are bioenergetic and healing.

I also believe that when we send out the energy that we're grateful for all we have, knowing that we'll always be taken care of, our body innately knows that it doesn't need to store fat because we trust that there will always be more food coming. That trust transfers into our body's ability to release our stored excess fat and disease-ridden cells. Our body simply knows what to do with our food when we're in the flow.

High-Octane Foods

There are so many amazing foods in our grocery stores and farmers' markets. If it grows from the earth and hasn't been processed or refined, then it's most likely a high-octane food.

A great tip is to stick to the outside edge of the grocery store when shopping, for the inside aisles contain the hidden, sneaky culprits. Not only are they much higher in price (because you're paying for packaging), they're also filled with substances that make our bodies shut down: sugar, hydrogenated fats, artificial sweeteners, preservatives, sodium, MSG, refined carbohydrates, and food coloring.

Our bodies need seven components to achieve maximum energy and vitality:

1. **Carbohydrates** are such an important macronutrient to consume each day, since they supply us with our vitamins, fiber, and antioxidants, and are our body's primary energy source. We must eat carbohydrates; in fact, they should make up approximately 40 percent of our diet. Choose natural, dark-colored, fibrous fruits and vegetables such as strawberries, blueberries, raspberries, grapefruit, lemons, apples, peaches, plums, green leafy vegetables (such as watercress, parsley, kale, lettuce, and spinach), tomatoes, broccoli, carrots, red cabbage, sweet potatoes, and zucchini. Also include whole grains, brown or wild rice, oatmeal, alfalfa, barley, wheatgrass, millet, beans, and legumes. Avoid white-colored carbohydrates such as white potatoes, white bread, white rice, white sugar, and white pasta, and almost anything that comes out of a box.

2. **Protein** supplies us with our essential amino acids, which are necessary for mental acuity, cellular repair, and a strong immune system. Enzymes are made of protein; our blood's hemoglobin is a protein; the structure of genes and brain cells is protein; and our skin, hair, nails, eyes, muscles, and hormones are mostly protein—which is why 30 to 40 percent of our daily intake should come from a lean, high-octane source that's usually "white" in color. These include chicken or turkey breast; halibut, trout, and sole; egg whites; whey and soy protein isolates; soybeans, soy milk, and tofu; flaxseeds and pumpkin seeds; and for those without milk allergies, skim milk, fat-free yogurt, and fat-free cottage cheese. Keep dark-colored proteins (red meat, egg yolks, cheese, and most cuts of pork) to a minimum.

3. **Essential fatty acids (EFAs).** Our bodies can't produce EFAs on their own, so it's absolutely imperative that we eat a small amount of these every day.

The two main essential fatty acids that we must consume daily are docosahexaenoic acid (DHA) and eicosapentaeonic acid (EPA), which come from omega-3 essential fatty acids. These EFAs comprise up to 50 percent of the total fat in the brain and central nervous system, so when we don't consume these powerful fats, our brains will stop working properly. We can get depressed and moody, and lose focus and concentration. EFAs aid in preventing age-related memory loss, dementia, Parkinson's disease, and Alzheimer's, as well as improving the central nervous system and cardiovascular health, relieving depression, PMS, and attention deficit disorder. EFAs also improve many skin disorders, such as eczema and psoriasis, and reduce blood pressure. In addition, they aid in the prevention of arthritis, lower cholesterol and triglyceride levels, and reduce the risk of blood-clot formation.

The best source of omega-3s are small cold-water fish, such as sardines, anchovies, or mackerel. Wild salmon is also an excellent choice, as are flaxseeds, flaxseed oil, and hempseed oil. Try to avoid the overconsumed omega-6 oils—safflower, corn, peanut, cottonseed, and sunflower—as they add little nutritional value and are only high in calories.

If you don't eat a small amount of the omega-3 food sources daily, I implore you to take an enteric-coated fish oil supplement with each meal. You should also have a tablespoon of cold-pressed extra-virgin olive oil daily (which is an omega-9 EFA). Canola oil, avocados, and certain nuts and seeds (such as peanuts—but not the oil—almonds, sunflower seeds, pumpkin seeds, and cashews), are also excellent sources for your EFAs. Keep in mind, however, that although EFAs are very "high octane," they're also very high in calories, so do limit your portions.

The fats that you want to try to steer clear of are the saturated and hydrogenated ones found in red meat, most dairy products (other than skim), fried foods, stick margarine, butter, and packaged items such as cookies, cakes, microwave popcorn, and crackers. These promote the inflammation and deterioration of brain cells and pack on the body fat. Anything containing the words *hydrogenated* or *partially hydrogenated* vegetable oil should be avoided.

4. Minerals regulate our bodies' acid-alkaline balance, hormonal and enzymatic activity, electrical movement in the nervous system, and oxygen transport. They're also necessary for developing and maintaining our bones, teeth, muscles, and all body parts. Minerals can't be made by the body, so they must be obtained from foods such as sea vegetables (including chlorella, spirulina, dulse, kombu, nori, wakame, and Irish moss), or with a supplement.

5. Vitamins are responsible for the metabolism of proteins, fats, and carbohydrates, and they're also responsible for building body tissues and for cellular energy exchanges. It's very important to eat a wide variety of fruits and veggies to get adequate amounts of all vitamins, but don't despair if you can't always eat right—at least start each day with a complete multivitamin/mineral supplement. (For more on supplements, please see page 112.)

6. Enzymes. Every bodily function is controlled by one or more of the body's 2,700 enzymes. For example, they're necessary for the breakdown, digestion, and assimilation of all our foods. Natural enzymes are found in fresh fruits and vegetables, as well as in fermented foods. However, microwaving, cooking, canning, and irradiating will destroy them.

Here are some signs that you may not be getting enough enzymes in your diet:

- Sleepiness after meals
- Excessive gas, belching, or burping after meals
- Longitudinal striations on fingernails
- Weak, peeling, or cracked fingernails
- Acne
- Undigested food in the stool
- Halitosis
- A bloated feeling after eating meat
- Nausea after taking supplements
- Multiple food allergies

- Constipation, diarrhea, or indigestion
- Chronic yeast infections

7. Water is the "fountain of youth"! Your body is approximately 70 to 75 percent water, so it's vital that you drink enough for all its functions, including movement, digestion, and temperature regulation. You must drink eight to ten glasses per day, and it's important to use the purest water available for drinking, cooking, and bathing. In this way, you'll prevent the absorption of pesticide residues, heavy metals (including lead from old plumbing), chlorine, and fluoride.

We Are What—and How Much—We Eat!

Now I'd like to throw a curveball into our understanding of energy. While we generally want to acquire the maximum amount, when it comes to food we actually want to *customize* the amount, since too much will make us heavy, depressed, and sick. The saying "less is more" really is the truth when it comes to eating.

Over the past few years, I've had the opportunity to work with one of North America's leading researchers, formulators, and lecturers in the field of optimal nutrition, Sam Graci. Sam is also the best-selling author of *The Food Connection* and *The Path to Phenomenal Health*. He formulated the award-winning superfood drink greens+, which, according to a study done at the University of Toronto, increases energy and vitality by up to 47 percent. Sam has also mentored me, teaching me much of what I know about the powerful effects of eating rich bioenergetic foods rather than processed and refined ones. The countless studies that he's provided me with over the years are proof that we're not just governed by our genetics—instead, it's what we eat!

One of the studies Sam showed me was done by Leonard Guarente, Ph.D., and Dr. David Sinclair, who found that a diet high in nutrients but low in calories (absolutely no junk food) would extend life and improve its quality so much that disease and illness could be obsolete. It seems that mice that consumed

30 percent fewer calories than what the average mouse ate lived an incredible 50 percent longer, virtually disease free! And in *Scientific American* in 1996, Dr. Richard Weindruch published his research "Nutrient Modulation of Gene Expression," which showed that by merely limiting the number of total calories eaten, the life span of a mouse could be extended by 40 percent. In human terms, that would translate into lengthening the predicted life span from today's average of 78 years to a healthy age of 95.

What can *you* do to reap these results? Well, if you ate about 10 to 12 calories a day (depending on how active you are) per pound of your ideal weight (in high-octane food), you'd live longer, with less chance of disease and sickness. For example, a woman with an ideal weight of 140 pounds should consume approximately 1,400 calories per day (140 x 10 = 1,400). However, what you don't want to do is get obsessed over counting calories or worrying. As soon as you turn this practice into pressure—feeling as if you're deprived or denied—your body goes into a fearful "starvation mode," not just physically but emotionally, so your energy drops and you begin gaining weight. Perhaps this is why American women get fat and French women don't. (According to Mireille Guiliano, in France—the home of cheese, chocolate, wine, and croissants—just 11 percent of the people have weight problems, compared to *67* percent in the United States.)

Your body will sense your worry when you've terrified yourself into "trying" to eat well. Whenever you "try" to accomplish something, you most often just create the opposite force within yourself and end up resisting what's happening. Your guilt of eating will do far more damage to your body than any food ever could. So instead, set a beautiful table; turn on some soft music; turn off your phones; give thanks for the meal that's about to nourish your entire body, mind, and soul; and *enjoy* it.

The simple fact is that your body is your temple. If the temple crumbles, your mind and soul will be held captive. The bricks and mortar of your physical body are made from the nutrients you put into it, and exercise will reinforce the integrity of the structure. Having said that, you can't just meditate and pray to manifest a healthy, strong, vital, energized body—you must take action. The secret is in learning to relax and trust in the process. For just as a seed knows with absolute certainty that the soil, rain, and sun will nourish it into a beautiful, strong oak tree, you must loosen up and know that when you nourish your body with healthy nutrients, pure water, sound sleep, loving movement, and conscious breathing, you'll grow into a strong, vital, and healthy woman.

Keep in mind that your stomach is approximately the size of your fist, so if you eat five small meals ("grazing") throughout the day, you'll be guaranteed to take in adequate amounts of carbohydrates, protein, essential fats, vitamins, minerals, and enzymes without overeating. The secret is to eat when you're hungry and stop when you're full . . . just as you must grieve when you're sad and rejoice when you're happy. Thank your body every day for doing the amazing job it does, and give it the nutrients it thrives on! Eating (or not eating) and exercise should never be done out of fear, self-loathing, or frustration. Instead, move your body because it works better when you do, eat healthy foods because you love yourself, drink water because your body thirsts for it, and breathe deeply to calm your mind and send your cells the messages that everything is precisely perfect.

The biggest lesson I've learned is to listen to my body. I know now that it really does have a knowingness, and it's been a long time since I've counted calories or stepped on a scale (something I used to do daily). The truth is that when I first began to take back my body, I needed to learn more about the foods I was eating and to discover what my natural "set point" was—but once I realized how much was too much and what the ideal amount was, I released my worry to count calories. And that's when I began to trust in the flow of life, believing that my body was a miraculous, self-healing machine that would never let me down. I honored it with rich bioenergetic foods, water, and herbal teas, and it began to honor me back. Sure, I'd occasionally have treats (such as sweets, wine, or decadent dinners), but instead of panicking, I listened. I ate slowly, savoring every bite, and the minute my body said, "Ah . . . that's enough!" I abided by it. I realized that I didn't have to eat the entire bag of chips or container of ice cream.

Not surprisingly, it was the times that I fell out of sync with myself—when I began letting my ego drive me—that I'd neurotically begin worrying that I was gaining weight. I wasn't, but my fears played tricks on me, whispering, "You're getting fat . . . you better start dieting!" And it was almost a guarantee that the minute I started stressing, fat started appearing.

Diets don't work simply because their very essence implies *die-ing*. Food is one of life's greatest offerings: It comes from the earth and is provided for us with absolutely every one of our needs in mind. And breaking bread together is a beautiful celebration of life, trust, loyalty, and companionship. So take joy in this blessing, but remember the distinction between satisfied and stuffed, reverence and indulgence, and respecting and punishing.

Supplementation

Although I absolutely know that our beliefs create our biology and that our body is a miraculous self-healing machine, we must still give it what it needs and not always what it wants! We must get our omega-3 essential fatty acids every day. We must give our bodies enough protein (67 percent of all women are deficient), and that may mean drinking a protein shake if we're not getting enough from our food. We must eat fresh, raw fruits and vegetables daily for fiber, vitamins, and minerals. And we must supplement with digestive-enzyme aids so that our bodies can absorb the vitamins and minerals from our foods. We can't close our minds to the enormous benefits of supplementation!

As I said in my first book, *Simply . . . Woman!*, I believe that the basis for optimal health at any age is a lean, well-nourished body. If we can achieve and maintain our ideal body weight and supply our bodies with healthy, nourishing foods, we can avoid many of the common ailments of today's society, the majority of which are caused by excess weight and poor nutritional habits. Now, we all know how difficult it can be to eat properly, especially when we're on the run, but some of us may forget that often the cravings we fall prey to are a *function* of our poor nutrition. That is, when the body doesn't have all the nutrients it needs, it sends out a signal to find them—to eat—and it isn't turned off until we supply the required nutrient.

We crave without realizing that our bodies are deficient in some vitamin or mineral. Unfortunately, if we grab a doughnut or a hamburger or some other convenience food that has very little nutritive value, we'll just want more and more. This then causes us to gain weight, which causes health (as well as self-esteem) problems, and a vicious cycle has begun. . . .

Under ideal conditions, we'd supply our bodies with optimal nutrition through our diet—unfortunately, that's not always possible. Thankfully, there's a convenient solution that can help even the busiest of us: supplements.

In the 19th century, our soils were rich in nutrients and minerals, so our plants were full of vitamins. Over the years, as crops were repeatedly planted, toiled, and harvested, the soil became depleted of its riches. Pesticides, fungicides, herbicides, and acid rain now pour down on our crops, and we're unaware that we're deprived of rich bioenergetic foods. Organic produce is still regarded as frivolous by many—in fact, most adults aren't even getting their recommended 8 to 12 servings of fruit and veggies each day! It's often these same people who refuse to believe that supplementation is necessary.

Ask yourself if you're getting your daily required vitamins, minerals, fiber, amino acids, and essential fatty acids. Then, before spending lots of money on vitamins and supplements, make the commitment to eat healthfully and drink a half a gallon of pure water daily.

Now, I recommend that everyone take a good-quality multivitamin daily, and always take vitamins and minerals with meals for better absorption. (And please note that supplements won't compensate for a poor diet.) Understand that even healthy people who eat well can still suffer from deficiencies or imbalances due to stress, lifestyle, diet, and illness, so if you're unsure about supplementation or if your vitamins are being properly absorbed, schedule a visit to your local naturopath or consult a nutritionist to have a proper assessment done. Also, take the time to research the company you're buying from.

I know that some people might have a difficult time affording supplements, but I wonder if they consider the incredibly important role vitamins play in maintaining health. Many feel that supplements seem ineffective, especially if they take one for a week or so and then expect to see or feel radical changes in their health. That's simply not the way they work. Baby steps over time create huge leaps and bounds, and I truly believe that along with a rich bioenergetic diet and pure water, vitamin supplementation is like a health-insurance policy.

I urge you to consider looking at your monthly expenses and creating a budget that will allow you to purchase these powerful health healers. But don't take them for fear that you'll die or age terribly without them—take them because you know your body thrives on them.

If you're under the age of 50, the following is a list of the ideal supplements that I recommend you take each day. (**Note:** I take and recommend a product called protect™, which is a powerful antioxidant capsule that contains the three supplements listed below.)

— **Three capsules of an antioxidant formula** (one at each meal), that contain vitamin A as mixed carotenoids, vitamin C as an ascorbate, selenium, n-acetyl-cysteine, lycopene, European bilberry, citrus bioflavonoids, and full-spectrum grape extract.

— **200 to 400 IU of vitamin E** (take half at breakfast and the other half at dinner). There's strong evidence that vitamin E may play a role in the prevention of heart disease, and it's especially needed for those with an underactive liver or gallbladder, or sufferers of diabetes, celiac disease, nerve damage, or muscle weakness.

— **50 to 100 mg of coenzyme Q10** (take half at breakfast and the other half at dinner). Aiding in the production of energy by our cells, this enzyme (also known as CoQ10) is often referred to as the "engine of the cell." It works synergistically with vitamins C and E and plays a major role in cell regeneration.

— **A high-quality multivitamin/mineral** (containing a minimum of 50 mg of your B vitamins). This is essential for those suffering from stress, fatigue, depression, PMS, and irritability, and it will also contain all of your essential minerals and vitamins in recommended amounts.

— **1,000 mg of calcium** (take half in the morning and the other half at bedtime). Calcium must be absorbed properly, so taking a digestive enzyme containing hydrochloric acid (see below) can help correct a deficiency. Calcium is especially important for those suffering from osteoporosis, brittle nails, muscle cramps, insomnia, and an irregular heartbeat. It also aids in weight loss.

— **500 mg of magnesium.** Aiding in energy production, glucose metabolism, and muscle and nerve impulses, magnesium is especially important for those who drink coffee, alcohol, or take prescription drugs.

— **A digestive enzyme with hydrochloric acid** (taken with meals). Proper digestion is where it all begins. After all, if we can't properly metabolize our foods, we won't be able to absorb the vitamins and minerals from them, let alone effectively digest them.

— **A 1,000-mg capsule of enteric-coated omega-3 essential fatty acids** (taken three times daily, one at each meal). You can also look for one containing borage oil for added heart health- and weight-maintenance benefits, but my favorites are o3mega+ joy (an enteric-coated EPA concentrate that actually improves your mood) and o3mega+glow (an enteric-coated EPA concentrate that's augmented with a unique selection of added ingredients to provide beautiful, glowing skin).

— **A high-quality green drink** to provide abundant energy and antioxidant support. You can look for one with added energy, detox properties, or multivitamin blends for extra benefit and convenience!

If you're over the age of 50 or notice the telltale signs of memory, vision, and/or hearing loss, I'd also recommend the following "age-defying" supplements:

— **50 to 100 additional mg of coenzyme Q10** (take half at breakfast and the half at dinner). A blood test will determine just how much more you need.

— **10 to 30 mg of dehydroepiandrosterone, or DHEA** (take under the tongue, half before breakfast and half before bed). Our "feel-good" hormone, DHEA helps with libido, metabolism, immune-system function, and controlling inflammation. (Be sure to have a blood test done to determine how much you need.)

— **.5 to 1.5 mg of melatonin** (take under the tongue, one hour before sleep). A natural hormone that regulates the body's biological clock and sleep cycles, melatonin is particularly important as we age because it is in deep sleep that our antiaging "growth hormone" is produced. It keeps us feeling young, fit, lean, and vital. (Be sure to use pharmaceutical grade, bioidentical hormones only under the supervision of your knowledgeable physician, and increase your amounts based on the results of your specific blood tests.)

We all know that there are many "magic" pills on the market, but I've personally had the greatest results with products from Genuine Health **(www.genuinehealth.com)**. Their items are of high quality, effective, safe, contain the most well-researched ingredients, and have won countless awards for having the highest standards. Nevertheless, please do your own research and become an educated consumer!

Every Breath You Take

From the moment we leave our "cocoon," we begin to breathe . . . always and everywhere. It's unfortunate that so many of us have lost touch with one of the most intimate things that we'll ever do. After all, it's through breath that we inhale each other, as well as the energy of all the people who have ever walked on this planet. The energies of Mother Teresa, Mohandas Gandhi, and even Buddha and Jesus Christ themselves are a part of what moves in and through us today. We're all connected, and until the moment of death, breath defines our life.

Most of us are completely unaware of our breathing, as it's an automatic process that happens within our bodies, something we don't need to be conscious of in order for it to transpire. The body is such a brilliant machine that it knows exactly how often to take a breath and how much air is needed to keep each organ functioning. It also knows instinctively when it's under attack and will enter into a "fight-or-flight" response mode.

The body identifies stress as anything that causes it to go into its primitive, automatic, survival mode. This fight-or-flight response happens as a result of worrying or due to an external circumstance that appears threatening. When this happens, a sequence of nerve cells firing occurs, and chemicals such as adrenaline, noradrenaline, and cortisol are released into the bloodstream. Breathing becomes rapid and shallow, as blood is shunted away from the digestive tract and into muscles and limbs, giving the body extra energy and fuel should it need to run or fight. Pupils dilate, vision narrows, impulses quicken, and the perception of pain diminishes. The body is prepared for battle—ready and waiting!

The trouble is that the fight-or-flight programming was hardwired into us millions of years ago, before multitasking, traffic jams, cell phones, laptops, and the information superhighway were created . . . that is, before stress was 24/7. Unfortunately, after 28 days of continued duress, our body reaches its point of burnout, and our adrenal glands can no longer handle the demands that have been placed upon them. Our fear has won over, and soon our shallow breathing, defensive nature, and short fuse become a normal part of our existence. We start to age, and we start to shut down. Disease, illness, obesity, and chronic fatigue take over, which are all just symptoms of tension.

However, by simply becoming aware of our breathing, we can slow down all the other stress responses in our body and allow ourselves to shift to a higher state of awareness. We can climb a ladder! (It's also important to note that this practice, along with prayer or meditation, is the only way to release our antiaging and feel-good hormone, DHEA, out into our bloodstream. DHEA is the only hormone to calm the raging response of stress on our bodies.)

Conscious Breathing

Conscious breathing is different from "yogic" or "meditation breathing" in that its strength and power lie simply in the mindful awareness of each breath. To powerfully anchor ourselves in the moment—to become the "I am"—we need to only abide by the sensations of each breath, one after another. You don't need to slow it down or speed it up . . . simply becoming aware of your breathing will create a path for transcendence. Remember: It's about *being,* not *trying.*

So, without interfering with your breathing pattern, notice the air as it travels in your nostrils and down into your lungs, and then back up and out again. Feel your abdomen and rib cage rise and fall. Notice your shoulders relaxing and your body becoming more at ease. Each mindful breath you take becomes a powerful and effective way for becoming centered.

Simply relax and allow your body to achieve ease and comfort. And with it, remind yourself of the divinity that flows through your body with each breath.

Every Move You Make

Sadly, I've watched so many women over the years exercise with self-punishment and self-loathing because they're so unhappy with their bodies and desperate to lose weight. They're not working out because they're honoring or celebrating their strength and vitality,

(Continued on page 118 . . .)

The Power of Your Z's

Sleep is the natural way to replenish your energy reserves, yet far too many of us are running ourselves ragged! After only a few nights without sufficient rest, changes in the immune and metabolic systems, as well as symptoms associated with premature aging (such as memory loss and glucose intolerance), may occur as levels of the stress hormone cortisol rise.

Daylight switches dopamine and cortisol on, while the darkness of nighttime turns them off and turns melatonin and growth hormone on. Allow me to explain in further detail what this means:

• **Growth hormone** is our anti-aging hormone, which keeps us feeling young, lean, strong, and healthy.

• **Dopamine** is the neurotransmitter that keeps us alert and vigilant. It controls the fight-or-flight mechanism that automatically alerts us in an emergency. It's released just before we wake, but if we go to sleep too late, it won't be released at all.

• **Melatonin** operates our "biological clock." Influencing so many things from fertility to insulin production to immunity, it's also our strongest anticancer hormone. Melatonin is produced from the neurotransmitter **serotonin,** which is made in our brain when we eat high-octane carbohydrates and the amino acid tryptophan. Serotonin is then converted to melatonin at sundown.

• Serotonin, dopamine, and melatonin must be kept in balance or **cortisol** levels will rise, and we'll experience depression, weight gain, premature aging, poor impulse control, irritability, lethargy, and negativity.

As you can see, along with eating well and exercising, sleep is one of the most important components of health and beauty . . . not to mention creativity, critical judgment, and even the ability to express yourself effectively. So get your Z's!

but because of a deep sense of fear . . . so they run, step, cycle, and pump, hoping to eradicate body fat and prevent it from ever coming back.

I go for a few long runs each week, as well as doing some Pilates, some occasional weight-lifting (my *Tight & Toned* workout DVD still works wonders for me), and a bit of yoga, but I never do any of it because of a disgust with myself over what I've eaten or because I'm terrified that I'll gain weight again. But I did exercise this way in the past—in fact, when I first started to work out, it was all about my outside image. I'd force myself to run faster . . . go longer . . . sweat more. I'd push my body hard with weights, straining tendons and ripping muscles.

Perhaps I'd been "bad"—maybe eaten foods I "shouldn't have" or drank a little too much wine—so I was going to have to pay for it through pain, deprivation, work, denial, or something I resented and wished I didn't have to do. But, hey, I was always taught "No pain, no gain." Looking back, I see such sorrow and survival in all those muscles that I'd built.

Then, somehow, as a shift in me began to occur, a shift in my view of exercise also occurred. I was beginning to live in Technicolor, and it was freedom! These days I often wake up, pull on my running shoes, saunter along outside, and just breathe while I talk to God and the world awakens around me. On other days, I pick it up into a light jog or motor along, running boldly with power and strength. But there are still many mornings that I cuddle up in bed for an extra half an hour. I listen to my body, mind, and soul, and honor all three.

What I do know for sure is that the days that I exercise are most often always good ones—strong, productive, and energized. And whenever I've let a few weeks go by without moving my body, I notice something missing. I'm less buoyant, and I feel heavier, both inside and out. But it isn't just the exercise that does it for me—it's exercising *outside* . . . hearing my feet hit the pavement . . . listening to the birds sing. It's breathing in the fresh air and noticing the beauty that surrounds me, no matter where I am in the world or what time of year it is. It's honoring nature and all life and reveling in how majestic the world is. It's giving thanks for my strong body, trusting that it will never forsake me.

My exercise has become a part of my spirituality. And whether I go down to the lake to stretch and look out across the mighty waves, or I run along the city streets early in the morning before the hustle and bustle begins, I'm always filled with this awesome sense that life is so amazing and that I'm a part of that amazement.

Exercising outside puts our bodies back in realignment. We've become so disconnected with the natural rhythms of the earth as we live, work, sleep, eat, and even exercise indoors. We need our daily intake of fresh air to gain the strength, wisdom, and stability of Mother Earth . . . to feel grounded in our lives.

There's no right or wrong way to move your body—the secret is moving it with love! Don't try so hard, just be. Find a few different ways to have fun with your body—experiment with dancing, walking, tai chi, yoga, swimming, running, qigong, martial arts, belly dancing, cycling, Pilates, stretching, weight lifting, skipping, even making love . . . the list is endless! No matter what you do, I call it "loving movement." In fact, there are many days that I turn on the music and just dance in my living room with reckless abandon. I couldn't care less who can see me (not that anyone can) as I come alive with passion and excitement. It's freedom, not punishment, to move my body!

I love to run (although I was never a runner until I was nearly 30—I didn't think I could ever run long distances), while flamenco dancing or kickboxing might be more your speed. The point is that you must find something you love! In the beginning, getting moving may feel difficult, which is normal. But just like pushing a car from a dead stop is tough, once it's in motion it's so much easier to keep it moving. Remember, movement creates momentum!

To this day, the first five minutes of my run is actually a stroll—I relax and let my body "drop in," and then—if and when I feel ready—I pick it up into a brisk walk. After about ten minutes, once everything seems to be in rhythm, I'll move into a jog. I go at whatever pace feels right that day. There's no competition—it's just me and the road. What's so funny is that within half an hour,

I'll most often find myself falling into the flow and picking up intensity. It's not punishment but rather empowerment!

Loving movement will lower your resting heart rate, blood pressure, and cholesterol. It will improve your immune and circulatory systems, as well as your posture, balance, strength, and vitality. It will send massive amounts of happy endorphins surging through your body and increase serotonin and growth hormone—not to mention that it will burn body fat and reduce pain, inflammation, arthritis, and chronic fatigue, all while giving you an overall sense of well-being. You'll feel strong, beautiful, and glowing . . . you will *shine!*

THE RAINDROP FELL ON THE GLISTENING LEAF . . .
SHE SIGHED WITH PEACE.
ALL WAS WELL.
EXACTLY AS IT SHOULD BE . . .
— Crystal Andrus

Chapter Five

The Power of Love

For most of my life, I thought that if I gave love, then that made me a loving person. I knew that I was supposedly loved by many people, but I rarely allowed myself to really receive anyone else's affection . . . to breathe it in and feel it wrapping around my heart, making me stronger with its softness. Because I was so afraid of being hurt, I seldom let anyone get even remotely close. I wasn't conscious of it, for I was in love with the *idea* of love, but up until the last few years, I don't think I even realized that other people could make me stronger. It was all about the power I felt when I gave to them and saw their own light shine brighter. I guess I'd counted on myself for so long that it never occurred to me that relationships were about more than my teaching and giving.

I think that even my marriage was based almost entirely on my helping my ex-husband—because as long as I was fixing him, I didn't have to fix myself. I thought that he needed me, and being needed was the closest thing I could associate with love. We'd gotten together as such scared and hurt kids that we'd defined and sculpted our relationship on those fears: "Don't go out without me. Don't look at her/him. Don't like things unless I like them. Don't leave me. Don't hurt me. Don't betray me. Don't have a life outside of me."

We lived in a bubble, and we made sure that neither one of us could get out of it. As I became a writer and speaker, there was no way that he was going to let me get on a plane to travel halfway around the world to share my message, just as there was no way I thought my marriage could survive my getting on one. Yet I'd given everything I possibly could to my marriage—including my voice and dreams—and I was beginning to feel as if I were drowning. I didn't want to leave my nest, but I didn't know how to stay there either.

The reality is that I didn't know how to speak my truth back then . . . to say what I really needed. And then one day, around my 30th birthday, this overwhelming voice in my head screamed at me: *This is it! If you don't do something right now, you're going to watch all your dreams pass you by!*

It's interesting that when my daughters were small, I painted this poem that I'd once read on the wall of their playroom:

For my dear children,
I wish for two things:
To give you roots,
And to give you wings.

I'd grown roots for myself, but I hadn't used my wings—and my girls were watching me, discovering what life was like for a woman. Although my husband and I did care so much about each other, we were far more afraid of not being loved and of being alone than we were in love. I could never fly as long as I stayed, and we both knew it.

It was the hardest thing I've ever done to leave him, and certainly not something I'm recommending to others. For me, it was an awakening: I was finally alone, for the first time in my life, to figure out who I was.

What I learned was that it wasn't everyone else I was most upset with, as I'd convinced myself it was—it was *me.* I was the most self-punishing person you'd ever meet. Dripping in shame and guilt, I had such a hard time letting go of my patterns, my past, and my inner demons. Now when I meet people who are very demanding of everyone else in their lives, I silently send them love because I know that they're actually toughest on themselves.

My kids will sometimes ask me, even to this day, if I still love their dad. And I can honestly tell them that I love him and always will. He was such an important person in my life—and besides, he's a part of them! How on earth could I not love him for helping to create my girls? They always smile and walk away, knowing that everything must be okay, even if I'm not married to their dad anymore.

I think that one of the worst things you can do to children's self-esteem is to condemn their parents in any way. Children internalize that criticism, equating their parents as parts of themselves—therefore, if one of their parents is "tainted," then they must be, too. Always remind yourself, and your children, that there's beauty in everyone! Besides, the truth is that the parts of others that we can't accept, or that infuriate us the most, are the parts of *ourselves* that we have yet to heal.

I chose my husband to help me confront the parts of myself I needed to make peace with—I just didn't know it at the time. As I continued on my own, I learned some pretty tough lessons about love and life. The most powerful one was that *you get what you give, but you can't give what you don't have.* At times I nearly flew back to the comfort of my old familiar nest, but I knew that I'd be going back for the wrong reasons. Until I had self-love and self-acceptance, I couldn't give honesty and trust to anyone. I could never accept anyone else for who they were until I learned how to accept *myself.* I might have been able to give others hope or some attention, but it wasn't until I was able to truly know love—from deep within—that I could transcend. It was then that extra-ordinary people began flocking into my life . . . that I was able to be loved. . . . that I felt the most beautiful I ever have!

Think about how many of us are searching for love, waiting for our "knight in shining armor." Yet he'll never come along unless we're resonating at the level of a princess! I'm not referring to the tiara she wears or the throne she sits on, but rather, her deep sense of knowing—she knows that she deserves to be loved and that she'll honor and treat her man like the prince he is, too.

Perhaps, truth be told, true everlasting love—the "soul-mate kind"—only happens once you've climbed to the top of your own ladder and have transcended your ego, when your soul is one with Divine grace and ready to finally come home. In other words, once *you* become the woman you're meant to be, then you'll know when you're with the person you were meant to be with!

Synchronicity

As soon as you start living in the moment, you'll begin to notice synchronicities happening around you regularly. Synchronicities are the people, places, or events that your soul attracts into your life to help you evolve, to increase awareness, or to resolve something necessary in your journey.

You may sometimes hear people mistakenly refer to synchronicity as coincidence, or two seemingly unrelated time/space events happening simultaneously—however, there are no coincidences in life. The famous Swiss psychologist Carl Jung was the first to coin the term *synchronicity,* describing it as a universal law that allowed humans a greater growth in consciousness.

All of us have experienced synchronicities, from dreaming about an old friend and then running in to her the next day to thinking about someone and then having him call you on the telephone. It can be as dramatic as experiencing severe financial difficulties and out of nowhere money seems to appear, or running into a stranger three times in the same day in totally unrelated places. It can be meeting a doctor who's an expert in a specific field, and then finding out two weeks later that your loved one is diagnosed with the exact illness that was this doctor's specialty.

As we begin to trust our intuition, we start to notice these synchronicities in abundance.

Attract Soul Supporters

You enter a room and are inexplicably drawn to a man you've never met. As you begin to chat with him, you experience a burst of energy or exhilaration that you can't describe. You're simply connected—synchronicity has brought the two of you together, and synergy is at work.

Synergy is when the sum of two things working together totals more than the sum of their individual parts. It most often happens when you meet someone and instantly bring out the best in each other.

Synergistic relationships happen every day, in all walks of life. From corporations merging to successful self-help programs such as Alcoholics Anonymous, world-champion sports teams, Grammy award–winning musical groups, or even two people falling in love... the list is endless.

Although finding someone with whom you'll have absolute synergy is rare (because both people must be highly calibrating and resonating at extreme levels of self-acceptance and love), it's incredible when it does happen. This connection between two perfectly aligned souls is often referred to as finding your "soul mate" or "kindred spirit." (But don't get caught up in the term *soul mate,* as it is so overused. It's more important that you simply understand that this ultimate synergistic union transpires on all levels between two people—sexually, emotionally, spiritually, physically, and intellectually.)

When we've found our soul mate, we're more powerful, confident, energized, enlightened, sexy, fearless, and beautiful with them than without. They make us better people, and we make them better, too. Our combined power equals far more than the sum of our individual parts. This doesn't mean that we won't sometimes disagree or that our personalities won't be different, but a soul-mate relationship will always survive the test of time.

A soul-mate union can't be enforced or manipulated. It simply is. *And fighting it is futile.*

While we've all experienced synergistic relationships that might not be soul-mate unions, they *are* incredibly meaningful and empowering. These people are our "soul supporters," and when we're with them, we feel an instant connectedness—a knowingness—and there's no mistaking it. And although we can't always understand our connection, we simply feel it. Our souls have attracted them into our lives for a reason—most likely, it's time for us to climb a ladder, heal an aspect of our consciousness, or make a shift in our awareness.

Soul supporters come in both sexes and in all races and religions, and they're necessary for our evolution. They may nurture, inspire, teach, guide, stimulate, calm, or even challenge us at times; and they might be around for a month or a lifetime—the duration is irrelevant. Sometimes people come along at a time when we're struggling for clarity, and during our interaction with them, the answers we've been searching for suddenly become so apparent. We're excited, even overjoyed.

Synchronicity brought these individuals into our lives at exactly the right moment—as the saying "When the student is ready, the teacher appears" alludes to—but our sudden clarity can often become clouded with fear and doubt. Afraid of losing them, we hold on tighter and try to make them be what we want them to be, yet true love needs no direction or control. Our soul understands this, knowing that once the healing has happened or our souls have evolved, these people may stay close by or drift off in another direction, and it has nothing to do with love.

As long as there's growth and learning, a relationship will sustain itself, yet all too often we start making plans about this person or relationship. Our ego needs to make sense of everything, to label everyone in its attempt to control, and we find ourselves trying to possess our soul supporters and define ourselves by the relationship.

The mind-made self can never understand the true reason you're attracted to someone, and very often you'll end up confusing it with something different from what it was intended to be. Ask yourself if you've ever pursued someone as a lover when perhaps he was meant to be a business partner or convinced a lover to go into business with you when he was never meant to share anything more than your heart. And then when the relationship doesn't work out the way you thought it should, you blame that person for not measuring up, when perhaps it was you who tried to control it in the first place. How many times have you held on to a relationship, job, friend, or lover longer than you should have, and then ended up resenting it, becoming angry and hurt when it's over?

Remind yourself that soul supporters are so for life, and always embrace those who once brought you a spark. Let them go when it's time, but know that you selected everyone in your life for a reason—the lesson is to understand why. Your outer world is always a healing tool to look at what's going on in your inner world. Soul supporters won't necessarily be the people who nod their heads and smile at everything you say and do . . . some of your greatest teachers, lovers, friends, and associates will actually be those who challenge you the most.

The Law of Attraction

Just as in the atom, the very basis of life—where highly vibrating protons attract highly vibrating electrons and low-vibrating protons attract low-vibrating electrons—we all attract the same frequency of energy that we emit. Positive attracts positive, and negative attracts negative. In other words, we attract what we are at the energetic level!

If you think negative thoughts about yourself, such as *I'm so ugly, no one thinks I'm attractive, I'll never find love,* then that's the thought pattern you're sending out into the Universe and that you'll ultimately attract back into your life. The important thing to realize is that you attract those whose energetic frequency resonates at a speed similar to your own. So, in essence, you attract the same kind of person that you are.

You may disagree and say, "No, I only seem to attract those who are totally the opposite of me." Well, that could be true, but what you might not realize is that your energetic frequency isn't the same as your personality. You see, your personality is the "identity" that you chose when you came to this earth in order for your soul to evolve (such as an outgoing personality or a shy one). You'll often attract opposite personalities because they're actually mirror reflections to help you see what you're not able to fully express in your own personality.

Your personality becomes a natural driver for your soul, not independent of it but rather a by-product of it. Your personality emerges thanks to many aspects, including how the planets were aligned at your birth, your name, your spiritual and earthly environment, your genetics, the messages you heard while growing up, and for what your soul needs in order to heal or evolve in this lifetime. It chooses the persona that it feels will best help its quest to transcend the ego and climb the ladders to enlightenment.

You may attract people into your life who have outgoing personalities and some shy ones, but what I can assure you of is that regardless of their personality type, these individuals' energy level most often resonates at roughly the same frequency as yours. Birds of a feather do flock together—although the more accurate saying should be "Opposites attract, but likes last."

For example, think about when you see a couple together who seems oddly matched: She's quiet, nervous, and reserved, while he's loud, boisterous, and aggressive. Keep in mind that no matter how they may appear to be on the outside, on the inside, each person probably feels quite at home—both resonating in fear, feeling insecure and scared. These two are "like lights."

If one person begins to heal an aspect of his or her consciousness and climbs a ladder, the relationship may begin to feel less comfortable, which will force one or both of them to then make a choice. Will one slide down a snake's tail to stay with the other? Or will the other choose to climb a ladder? Will one dim their light, or will the other brighten up?

The gift is in learning why we chose the relationships that we have, and then to learn and grow from them. Yet all too often, instead of learning the lesson and healing ourselves through the gifts these teachers have offered us, we find ourselves repeating patterns, falling into one love affair after another that leaves us feeling frustrated and alone, wondering why we find ourselves attracting the same kind of people over and over. We can't understand why we once adored these individuals but soon became repelled by them.

It's almost like being on *Snakes and Ladders:* We climb a ladder, then move two spaces, land on a snake's tail, and begin all over again. Just think of how many women have traded in one husband only to find themselves in the same boat five years later!

Facing Yourself

For years I couldn't figure out why it was that I was so "together," yet I always attracted "messed-up" people—especially wild and crazy friends who loved to party even though I rarely went out. Although I did have some really lovely "true blues" whom I'd been friends with since my teens, and who brought gentleness and security into my life, it was always the most outrageous individuals whom I seemed to devote most of my time to.

Convinced that I was a fixer, I believed that God was sending these people to me so that I could help them. And I did help them most of the time, but often that fixing came with a price. The frustration it would cause my ex-husband, and subsequently myself, was sometimes unbearable. I'd get calls at three in the morning from a drunken friend who was having a great time and just felt like hearing my voice, or I'd have another one sitting in my living room at breakfast time, sobbing over a cup of coffee. My husband had no tolerance for mixed-up people, especially if they were counting on me—and if I were entirely honest, after months of being the fixer, I'd often grow frustrated with them, too. It wasn't until I began to do work on myself that I realized I was attracting people into my life whom the Universe was sending to help me see what it was I needed to heal *in myself.*

I started thinking about the parts of my consciousness that I needed to heal, and that's when I realized that what we fear will appear. *My* greatest fear was being regarded like these friends of mine—most of them were exactly what my "nun" would insist were the worst things a woman could be and do. To drink, party, be promiscuous, and act crazy, loud, and daring was *unacceptable!* And my own repressed fears created a dynamic in which I continued to attract the very kind of woman I resisted within myself.

The next step remained healing this within me, so I started by writing out my learned beliefs. My mother had been raised by very strict Pentecostal parents who believed that dancing, drinking, and most things sexual—including masturbation and premarital sex—were mortal sins. She was also taught never to share her "dirty laundry" with anyone. Secrets were meant to be kept secrets! And as much as my own mother rebelled against those rules, she still believed them at her deepest core. So her learned beliefs became mine, and her inner struggles became mine. And we both spent much of our lives fighting against the very core of who we were.

My work had begun . . . I knew that I needed to heal this part of myself, especially since I had my own childhood demons racing inside of me. I had my own secrets and shame that I needed to release. As I began to step out of my perceptions of the truth and began looking at my beliefs from different perspectives, an unbelievable shift happened in me. It was like an instant healing, and the light immediately turned on. I got it! This wasn't about me or my friends being wild and crazy—it was about my judgments and fears about what being wild and crazy meant. It was my self-repressed shame that deep down I'd been wild and crazy in my teens, and I was terrified that anyone would find out about it. My attachment to my perceptions of truth, of what a "good woman" should be, was keeping me captive in my own fear and guilt.

The more I began to uncover my beliefs and then reevaluate them to see if they were serving me any longer, the easier it was to see that this constant internal battle wasn't really God and the devil at war within me, as I'd been taught to believe. The only battle was me fighting my beliefs . . . it was me fighting me.

As I began to own my thoughts, feelings, needs, and desires and redefined my concepts about love, men, sex, and having a good time—gently explaining them to my nun, telling her that good and evil are only perceptions that we're taught to believe—I was able to embrace the wild woman hidden deep inside of me. And amazingly, as I stopped resisting myself and all of my judgments, my nun stopped persisting! A weight was lifted—I stopped fighting myself and just accepted myself for who I was: spiritual and sexual . . . enlightened and worldly . . . intelligent and goofy. I was calm, serene, accepting, and exuberant. I was everything and nothing.

I certainly didn't become a mixed-up party girl (although I did become far less uptight about having a glass of wine or dancing the night away), but what I did become was far more gentle and accepting of myself and everyone else in my life. My job wasn't to fix anyone—it was to love them regardless.

What was most interesting in all of this is that once I began to accept all of me, my neurotically crazy friends seemed to wander off in search of new, more dramatic friendships, and the faithful few friends who did stick around seemed so much tamer than they used to be. *Hmm,* I wondered, *who's really changing here?*

I believe that this is what we call "projection"—that is, I projected my own fears, issues, and hang-ups on others and make it about them, rather than me. Not surprisingly, within no time I began attracting new friendships with women who were exactly as I was: confident, content, successful, accepting, fun, serious, logical, witty, silly, proper, intelligent, mature, and carefree.

What's so amazing is that anyone can climb a ladder at any given time, and once they've scaled it, they don't ever have to return to where they once were. We should never judge someone based on their past or because of their family or assume that the "lowest lights" can't instantly be turned up.

Remember that when we can't accept others for their so-called faults (or we only notice all the quirks and things they need to change), it just means that we haven't yet learned to accept *ourselves* for those same qualities. As I explained to a client the other day, when we change one part of an equation, we change the outcome. So if we stay focused on trying to change our partners (which is impossible, since we can never change anybody else), our end result will always be the same: We'll remain frustrated and upset. For true change to happen, we must change *our* part of the equation, which will then change the outcome, which will then motivate our partners (usually unconsciously) to make changes within themselves. The more that others can hurt, disturb, or frustrate us just means the more healing we still need for ourselves.

As I explained in *Simply . . . Woman!* when other people upset us, it's never about them, but rather a feeling that they've triggered in us, which we'd do almost anything to avoid, even if it means self-sabotage. But once we discover and face our greatest fears—our own issues of rejection, unworthiness, and disapproval—and we learn to like ourselves regardless of what anyone else thinks, we begin to celebrate our differences and accept others for theirs, too. We learn to "live and let live."

To be a fully integrated person—to be the "I am" and transcend the ego—we must learn to accept all parts of ourselves and know that the Divine gave us every feeling we have and every thought we think. Once we accept ourselves, we can stop trying to change ourselves and become the women we were always meant to be. We'll feel the shift in our resonance, and we'll never want to go back to that dark and fearful place!

Consciously Evolving

In our quest for transcendent beauty, we must consciously practice the art of aligning our energies with the highest levels of human consciousness—of aligning our personalities with our souls. We can't fear change . . . evolving . . . or meeting new people. We can't worry that our relationships won't survive if we reach for our dreams or that we won't have the willpower to be "good." We can't be afraid!

What we must be is wise about the rush we get from certain energies, and to step away to recenter and make sense of it. Sometimes we're overwhelmed in a new situation because it all seems so exciting: We mistake lust as love (or vice versa), or our ego starts whispering into our ear that the grass is greener over there . . . just because *it's* never content. When our ego steps in, we instantly downshift to a lower resonance and can't seem to make sense of what's right—and that's when we begin to fool ourselves.

But sometimes the attraction is exactly what your soul knows you need in order for your life to evolve. When you meet someone new, ask yourself: "Does this feel right? Do I feel like I've known this person for a thousand years and I'm finally coming home? Do I feel most like 'me' when I'm with him or her?"

The movie *Jurassic Park* described life—or energy—as something that always finds a way. We may try to bury it, squash it, or douse it, but it will never die. Try as we may, on some level we can't deny what's really there because it's all around us. Our soul knows exactly where and how we're meant to live, and our Higher Power will continually send us the people we need to help light our way!

When we fight what is and try to make things
what we want them to be, we live with an internal emptiness.
Passion is the oil to our lamp. Without it, our soul starves.

Haven't you ever felt so enthralled by someone that the more you try to stop thinking of him, the more he takes over your entire thoughts? Sometimes all it takes is acknowledging the attraction and then allowing yourself to accept and feel it, without necessarily acting on it. Denying an attraction only makes it more enticing—the more you resist (or stress about it), the more power it gains over you. Before you act on any "temptation," allow it to sit inside of you without judgment, and ask yourself what the feeling is telling you about your inner self. In other words, is this a ladder or a snake's tail?

Sometimes you'll find yourself attracted to someone simply because the Universe guided him to you and you met him at a time when his energy was brimming and yours was low. He helped shine some light on you, so you suddenly felt a little brighter. Other times you've attracted another to show you the parts of yourself you still need to accept. So the secret in your quest for absolute energy and ultimately transcendent beauty is to rise above the immediate rush you get from someone and clearly assess what he's meant to be in your life. The ego can play tricks on you if you let it!

What you can't do, however, is allow yourself to be afraid of connecting with others . . . for whatever reason. When you do, you essentially hold yourself back from necessary evolution. Living in a bubble and avoiding those who seem too exciting or intense may sound like the safe and sensible bet, but one day when the bubble breaks (as it typically does), you'll be left feeling insecure, resentful, and even filled with self-doubt. Besides, living in a bubble implies that you're living with fear, and a fear-driven life will never feel abundant, joyous, or beautiful.

Déjà Vu

Déjà vu is French for "already seen." That is, it's an uncanny feeling or illusion of having already seen or done something that's actually being experienced for the first time. There are a few different types of déjà vu; however, for simplicity's sake, we're going to address the one that most people have experienced—those odd and rare moments when the present feels like the past . . . when you feel as if *I've done this before!*

No one can actually explain what's happening when we experience déjà vu, but I believe that when it occurs, it's a special gift from the Universe that allows us to become *acutely* aware of the present. Everything seems to slow down, as this special blessing is a wake-up call to point out a significant person (or people), an event, or surrounding, which is especially important to our personal journey. Déjà vu often happens when we're highly calibrating, and it's a sign that a spirit guide or angel is close by. Most important, it teaches us to value the here-and-now.

If you're lucky enough to experience déjà vu, give thanks

for the opening of your eyes to something or someone very important that you're meant to take particular notice of.

The reality is that no matter how dim others' lights are, they can never lower yours unless you give your power away. Think of it this way: If you were to enter a pitch black room and turn on a flashlight, the dark could never dim the light, but the light will always brighten the darkness! Remember that Jesus himself spent his life around lower lights knowing that they could never steal his, saying: "I am the way, the truth, and the light." He didn't say that he was *trying* to be—he just knew that he was.

Identify Energy Drainers

I absolutely do believe that if we stay in our most powerful place—always abiding by our soul—then no one can ever take our power from us. However, until we've transcended the ego (which is a lifelong quest), then at times we're going to fall. And when we do, we can easily let an energy drainer zap us if we don't know how to keep our light protected!

The gift that highly intuitive people possess is that they can instantly feel others' energy as soon they come into their presence, almost as easily as turning on the car's defroster on a cold winter's morning. Voilà—instant clarity.

Now, most of us have a gut instinct that intuitively tells us if something or someone is right for us. Unfortunately, though, says Malcolm Gladwell, best-selling author of the fascinating book, *Blink:*

> We live in a world that assumes that the quality of a decision is directly related to the time and effort that went into making it. When doctors are faced with a difficult diagnosis, they order more tests, and when we are uncertain about what we hear, we ask for a second opinion. And what do we tell our children? Haste makes waste. Look before you leap. Stop and *think*. Don't judge a book by its cover. We believe that we are always better off gathering as much information as possible and spending as

> much time as possible in deliberation. We really only trust conscious decision making. But there are moments, particularly in times of stress, when haste does not make waste, when our snap judgments and first impressions can offer a much better means of making sense of the world.

In other words, don't try, don't think, don't second-guess—*just be!* Feel your body talking to you and trust its message. If you sense that something's off, trust it. And remember that I'm referring to your intuition here, which is something you can easily develop. In fact, there are many wonderful books dedicated to helping you do just that.

One of the simplest ways to develop your intuition is to become aware of your own physical warning signs and trusting that your feelings are right. Think back: Have you ever begun chatting with someone and within minutes you just knew that something was off—that you simply didn't connect? You weren't sure why and might have even thought that it was something you did. Perhaps you experienced a feeling of uneasiness or the opposite (an overload of frenetic energy), but the longer you hung around, the more uncomfortable you became. Maybe you felt your throat or upper chest tightening up, or it hurt to swallow (that's why we often refer to energy drainers as "vampires"). You might have felt disoriented, sensed an overwhelming pressure building in your brain, been unable to think straight, or become very tired.

Become cognizant of these reactions in your own body, and soon you'll zoom in quickly! You'll realize the moment that you must put up your glass wall, silently acknowledge to yourself that something about this encounter isn't working, say a prayer of protection, and take a moment to graciously step away and get recentered. The reality is if you learn to listen to the split-second feeling you get when you first see someone, you'll almost never be lead wrong. But there's a catch: It only works with 100 percent accuracy as long as you're abiding by your soul—the minute you step into your ego, the message becomes skewed.

Feeling drained does happen, sometimes even with soul supporters—especially if you try to talk to them when they're tired or totally distracted, or after a conversation has simply gone on longer than it naturally should have. You've got to pay attention to the nonverbal signals that they may be displaying, such as crossed arms, avoiding eye contact, turning their bodies sideways, or sudden restlessness. By ignoring these signs and trying to force an interaction, you'll inevitably set yourself (and them) up for a negative exchange, from which you'll most often leave feeling drained and even upset. If this continually happens with the same person, you're just not aligned, and you need to accept it. It might be because of one of your own issues or something they're carrying around—don't worry about it or take it personally.

Occasionally feeling "off," on the other hand, is very different from being around an energy drainer. An easy way to understand the difference of being around a soul supporter with that of an energy drainer is when you've stayed awake an entire night in a magical conversation with someone who leaves you feeling passionate and alive, compared with a few minutes of talking to someone whom you dread seeing again.

But don't be too hard on them! These aren't bad people—their light is just not as bright as yours, and they're simply drawn to you, wanting what you have, not realizing that they must find it from within. They may try to pull you into their drama—or their "unconscious control maneuvers"—unknowingly trying to raise their own level of energy by taking yours.

We all have unconscious control maneuvers, but low-calibrating people depend upon them to make themselves feel better. These maneuvers are the dramas or themes they take on to try to obtain energy from outside of them. For example, have you ever picked up the phone, only to hear the voice of that whiny old friend who's never happy and always hopes that you'll cheer her up, and you'd do anything to escape the call? How about the co-worker who gossips constantly in her attempt to make herself feel better about her own insecurities by putting others down? What about the controlling boss who relentlessly criticizes you to feel more powerful by making you feel weaker?

Then there are the relatives who never quite let us into their world. Their vague answers and detached manner causes us to work hard at trying to win them over, all the while wondering, *What's wrong with me? Why don't they like me?* And there are the passive-aggressive people who smile at us as they make digs—cutting up our outfit or hairstyle under the shadow of concern or love—although the worst unconscious control maneuvers are often displayed by the overtly aggressive, authoritative people who use direct control and force to suck the life out of us. If we let them do so, we're left with feelings of self-doubt and low self-esteem.

The truth is that not only have we all been on the receiving end of these behaviors—and we've been guilty of one or more of them in our time, too—but in our quest to live with transcendent beauty, we must learn how to recognize when we're creating drama or being dealt one, and stop it!

Although energy drainers are usually pretty obvious (negative, gossipy, depressed, victimized, defensive, or angry people), there are times when you may feel drained even when you're around someone who's considered by others to be enlightened or soulful. This can sometimes be baffling when you meet this apparently wonderful person and your body begins sending you warning signs that something is off. Realize that unless you're constantly "in check"—abiding by your soul—you may have triggered something in them, or they in you, and one of you has entered into an unconscious control maneuver. In other words, someone's ego is screaming to be heard.

This can be overcome if you continue to stay in the soul. If you don't, then within seconds you'll unknowingly shift down to a lower-resonating frequency, as seen with emotions of pride, insecurity, jealousy, frustration, envy, control, contempt, defensiveness, self-righteousness, and anger (more on them in the next chapter), and you'll immediately feel a heaviness come over you. Maybe your head will start to pound or your chest will tighten up. You'll leave feeling rotten, wondering what went wrong. *Well, you've allowed yourself to dim your own light.*

The easiest way to know if you're the "drainer" or the "drainee" is to ask yourself: "Which 'self' am I serving? Am I defensive or totally open to this person?" If you know that you're absolutely centered and abiding by your higher self, but the conversation is just too difficult for you to maintain, then that's your sign that you're in the presence of an energy drainer.

It's key to remind ourselves that we can only be drained if we allow ourselves to be pulled into others' unconscious control maneuvers. I know that this can be very difficult when we're constantly around people who are lower lights than we are. It's easy to say that if we just elevate our own level of energy, to choose to resonate with love and peace, then no one can ever make us do anything that might lower our integrity. But the truth is that no matter how loving we may be, very few of us have the resolve and inner personal power to always be fearless, truthful, kind, and unstoppable—to keep resonating at a state of beautiful bliss.

So until you feel strong enough to be able to perpetually stand powerful—to stay in a place of love and light—choose your company well. Just as you protect your children and try to keep them around positive people because of peer pressure, do the same for yourself. Now, that doesn't mean that you should snub anyone or alienate others, but rather, know when to step away and refuel—to keep your light radiant and glowing! And always be gracious and kind when you're retreating into your place of protection.

As you become more aware of your own inner resonance, you'll feel the energy shift as it occurs in your body. It can shift from day to day, sometimes even hour to hour. For those of you who are on an emotional roller coaster and haven't learned how to maintain a heightened level of awareness, the shift can be rather dramatic and can leave you feeling as though you have manic depression. But once you begin to transcend the ego and your soul is revealed, the balance will become easier, and one day you'll suddenly realize you that you're no longer trying to feel good or be joyous . . . you've simply *become* joy in all that you do.

Be What It Is You Need

I was doing a coaching session the other day with a new client, Angelina. As we spoke for the first time, I could feel her sadness through the telephone. Her voice was meek and quiet, and she was lonely and unsure. Having come from Spain to marry a successful American businessman, Angelina was in a new country with no family or friends, and she felt that his family looked down on her. She'd just had her second baby and was feeling totally isolated and very depressed, especially since she'd gained a lot of weight in her pregnancies. Her new husband was too busy most of the time for her and the kids. And since their sex life was almost negligent, she felt totally unattractive.

Before we went on, I told Angelina that I could imagine her with beautiful long hair, wearing a flowing dress and looking like a goddess. She cried harder and said that she *was* very beautiful before gaining so much weight, and she did have long, wavy black hair but had recently cut it. I insisted that she was still beautiful and that the only way the world would see it was once she started seeing it herself!

Next, I asked, "What is it that you need in your life right now to feel happier?"

Angelina told me that she needed a friend and to go out more. She needed her sister-in-laws to like her and invite her out

Trust Your Vibes

John Gottman, Ph.D. (aka "the love doctor" and author of the fascinating book *The Mathematics of Marriage*), points out that the majority of couples who are still happily married for longer than 15 years tend to recall a positive experience regarding their very first interaction with each other. These couples just knew that something "felt right," *right from the beginning!* (Malcolm Gladwell goes on to explain this instantaneous "knowingness"—as something he calls "thin-slicing"—in his book *Blink.*)

If we're absolutely honest, most of us who have gone through a divorce or bad breakup would confess that our first instinct when we met our ex told us, "Hmm . . . maybe not." Unfortunately, most women are pleasers and seek approval—even if that means winning over the very person we intuitively know isn't right for us!

I'd like to share an amazing technique with you, which I have many of my clients do to increase their intuition and learn how to start trusting in their gut instinct again, particularly when it comes to attracting and choosing the people in their lives. I call it the "Three-Second Assessment," and it's incredibly simple: Just sit for an hour in a busy mall or park or even on a street, and the minute you spot someone intriguing, ask yourself, *Who is this person?* Then let your instincts talk. Without reservation, allow yourself to *feel* everything you can about this person—try not to think. Naturally, your feelings will come to you as thoughts, but they'll be guided by your intuition, rather than your logic. This exercise requires you to simply trust in your feelings, but it doesn't oblige you to act upon them.

I often practice this if I'm sitting in an airport or when I'm out running. I can sense within three seconds if others are innately happy, sad, angry, frustrated—in other words, the intensity of their light. And more important, I know if these people are "right" for me. Because that's the key: *Are they right for you personally?*

Start trusting in your vibes again. Listen to that voice that warns "No!" instead of trying to convince yourself that you can win certain individuals over, or that maybe you're being unfair or too hard on them. There are millions of humans in the world, so why not choose one who really feels right for you?

Now, having said that, I'd like to stress that it's important not to regret your past relationships—every one of them was a learning experience. The gift in this exercise is to simply start listening to your higher self again. The signs are always there.

to coffee with them. She needed her husband to want to make love to her, and she'd like to start her own business. She needed her family to support her, and she needed to lose weight . . . to feel beautiful again.

I told her that we teach people how to treat us, and I asked her if she could first be those things to herself. In a split second, her resonance shifted, and she said in her sweet Spanish accent, "Ah . . . I see. I need to first be a friend to me."

For the remainder of the call, we came up with ways that over the next week she could be good to herself and treat herself with love, kindness, respect, and dignity—how she could be a friend to herself. She realized that we attract what we emit, and she was emitting such negativity that she wondered why *anyone* would have wanted to spend time with her.

Angelina decided that she was going to join her local gym, which would help her lose the weight, meet some women in her neighborhood, and start getting out more. She also decided that she'd book herself into a spa for an afternoon of pampering. And then just before we hung up, I asked her if I could pull a card from Doreen Virtue's *Goddess Guidance Oracle* deck.

I spread the cards facedown on my table, and pulled out one labeled "Eireen, the Goddess of Peace." I described the card to Angelina, explaining how Eireen was standing in a beautiful white dress with long black hair falling down around her shoulders, holding a baby in one arm, with dolphins dancing in the ocean behind her. The card looked exactly as I'd pictured my new beautiful client.

"There is no need to worry," I read from the card. "Everything is going to work out."

Five days later, Angelina called me up to say, "Oh, Crystal, I can't believe that so much has changed in my life in only one week! My husband was so happy that I joined the gym, and I already feel so much better. I've made some friends, and I love doing the salsa-dancing aerobics class. Then last night as I was getting ready to go for a bike ride, he said that he'd come, too—I never even had to ask him! We put both the babies in the bike seats, and off we went. The smell of the ocean reminded me of home . . . I haven't felt that alive since I left Spain! But the best part is that when we got home, we made love for the first time in 19 months."

I squealed and repeated my earlier message to her: In order for our outer world to change, we must change our inner!

As the amazing Debbie Ford says in *The Dark Side of the Light Chasers:*

> The world mirrors yourself back to you. If you love, nourish, and appreciate yourself internally it will show up in your external life. If you want more love, give more love to yourself. If you want acceptance, accept yourself. I promise that if you love and respect yourself from the deepest place of your being, you will

call forth that same level of love and respect from the universe. If you think you are doing this and your external world does not look like you think it should, I ask you to look inside one more time. Uncover the lie. Uncover what you are not allowing yourself to have, what you most desire.

Or as I keep saying: Fake it till you make it!

The Soul of Sex

Although we're spiritual beings, we can't forget the power and importance of our human experiences! Our Higher Power created us in human form to understand parts of itself that it couldn't as a spiritual being—and sex is one of the most loving ways of honoring our bodies and each other. Soul-driven sex is next to godliness, and a sexually confident woman simply has a walk, a talk, and a look that tells the world that she loves who she is.

When we're in the "soul of sex," it becomes an immensely powerful connection, not a

The Art of Flirtation

Don't think you're a flirt? Think again! Anthropological research shows that flirting happens in all cultures and societies around the world. Most of us think of it as something a teenage girl does with a cute boy, but it's actually the most basic and natural language that we *all* instinctively know. Babies do it with their mothers, little girls do it with their grandfathers, and old ladies harmlessly do it with handsome young men. And we do it when we smile, tilt our heads down, and look up wide-eyed and innocent. A good flirt is playful, lighthearted, and giving. (And a great smile is an added bonus—a great reason for taking care of your teeth!)

Many of us don't realize it, but verbal communication only amounts to about 7 percent of the way we express ourselves, whereas our body language tells over 50 percent of how we're really feeling (38 percent comes from *how* we speak). So one of the most inviting things we can do with anyone is to engage them in a game of natural healthy flirtation.

Instead of thinking about the sexual connotations associated with flirting, let's imagine it as "attention without intention!" After all, we each want to feel appreciated and acknowledged. Some call it stroking the ego, but the truth is that an honest flirt is someone who can give a compliment freely and comfortably and isn't dictated by his or her own ego and pride. The greatest natural salespeople in the world have mastered the art of persuasion, and most of it comes from harmless and gentle flirtation.

Now a word to the wise: Never flirt (not even harmlessly) with a man who's with a woman—or, for that matter, never flirt with your friend's man!

performance or duty, but one where we become stronger because of each other. The soul of sex is accepting, allowing, carefree, confident, generous, erotic, giving, gracious, honest, inspired, joyful, kind, liberating, natural, nurturing, open, patient, receiving, satisfying, serving, spiritual, surrendering, tender, trusting, unrepressed, unselfish, virtuous, warm, and willing!

Sadly, some people degrade and demonize the act as something dirty and shameful, but soul-driven sex can never be wrong. Sexual energy is part of what drives us, so to ignore our sexuality is to neglect a part of our life-giving force. To deny ourselves the right to enjoy this most basic human need is actually self-punishing.

For those of you who struggle with allowing yourself to release and surrender to the soul of sex, it's essential to reevaluate your beliefs and attachment to it. What messages did you grow up hearing about sex? Was it a life-giving celebration or a duty? From what you saw, how comfortable were your parents with their bodies? How comfortable are *you* with your own body and with your partner's body? Do you have hang-ups or insecurities about sexuality as a whole?

More important than how often you have intercourse, how long you have it for, or how crazy your sex life is, soulful sex can only happen when you express your truest, most honest needs, thoughts, fantasies, and desires with freedom. It's speaking your truth that will allow you to feel at home—to be able to love and be loved—without judgment or shame (which also means that you must allow your partner to share his deepest thoughts and truths, too). When you become jealous, self-righteous, or condemning, you end up stepping into the fear-driven mind of the ego, and you'll destroy your chances of ever knowing true love and intimacy.

Although sexual synergy is one of life's most powerful connections, don't ever misinterpret meaningless intercourse as coming from the soul. One-night stands or seductive performance-driven sex may feel good at the time—and may even make you feel better about *yourself* temporarily—but the long-term negative side effects can be devastating. If sex is ego driven (that is, about trying to fill a void, numb pain, or make someone love you), then in the end, you're going to feel absolutely left in the dark. As clichéd as it sounds, sex truly is about the body-mind-spirit connection—if you're not in a meaningful relationship with a soul supporter, having it with "just anyone" can bring about agony.

Also, if the act is always about what you need to create outside of yourself—that is, what you need to look like, wear, use, watch, drink, imagine, control, manipulate, or receive—then sex will inevitably become empty because your ego can never be satisfied. Since outcome rarely matches expectation, the idea of what could be is never fulfilled, thus the reason for most addictions, whether to pornography, drugs, or alcohol. Not that having fun with what you wear, watch, do, use, or imagine is wrong . . . it's not. It's just that if you think you *need* something, then it owns you rather than your owning it. You're not having fun with your love life, you're controlled by it.

When you have to control it, change it, talk about it, analyze it, wish it were "like this" or "like that," then you're in the ego. And when you believe that who you are sexually defines you, protects you, or makes you more acceptable to the world, it's your mask—your false courage.

So celebrate your body and be in the now! Kiss as though you'd never kissed before. Let your lover touch and explore you without worry, distraction, or wanting to direct or control—instead, just receive and give love as a willing participant, knowing that he's showering you with his energy and vice versa. And breathe it in—*it's pure beauty.*

Love All Your Parts

In order for you to experience the soul of sex, it's imperative that you learn to love all of your body parts. Women have been living in shame for far too long. This shame is totally unfounded, since it goes right back to our earliest beginnings in a patriarchal world that has whispered negative messages into our ears for as long as we can remember. In Eve Ensler's controversial, slightly angry, yet important book *The Vagina Monologues,* she shares how countless women, especially those in the older generation, have sadly never explored their own bodies, achieved an orgasm, or discovered what most excites them sexually.

In order to enjoy sex and shine in all its glory, we must appreciate the beauty of our bodies . . . and of *all* bodies. The reason it's called sex is because it's sexy! Sadly, however, many women grew up not knowing, loving, or honoring all their parts. Most never talked about their vaginas, looked at their vaginas, or even used the word *vagina.* In my home, for example, we'd say that we had a problem "down there," and we'd say it red faced, embarrassingly looking toward the floor.

If you believe that anything about your body is unattractive, or you're too embarrassed to look at it with love, too ashamed to explore and satisfy it, or too nervous to let your lover ravage every inch of you, then it's time for you to go back and reevaluate your learned beliefs. You must redefine your concept of what's sexy to make it fit *you!*

If you're uncomfortable with nudity or have a difficult time enjoying yourself, the time has come to rediscover the human body and look at it through the eyes of the soul. If you don't desire sex or you shut down when your mate approaches you, you need to do the work of uncovering the emotional pain that's keeping you stuck. What are you most afraid of? What is it that your ego starts whispering into your ear? What are you losing by letting yourself miss out on one of the most powerful and fulfilling things you can give to yourself?

Take time to get back in touch with *you.* Spend time alone . . . naked. Have long baths. Cream your skin with beautiful lotions, shave your legs, and love your body by learning how to pleasure it. And maybe it's even time to get out a mirror and get familiar with every single inch of you! You need to be comfortable in your own skin, and then when you're with your lover, remind yourself that he's there to honor and celebrate you, as you are him. It's not about perfect breasts, a firm tummy, or a perky butt—empowering, soul-driven sex happens when you're totally present in the moment, and you allow yourself to just *be*.

See her. . .
Embrace her . . .
Love her . . .
She is you.
Beautiful . . . in all your glory.
— Crystal Andrus

The Ten Ego-Driven Destroyers of Beauty

There are innumerable and obvious destructive actions, emotions, and attitudes that will shift your energy to a stagnant and negative place, such as racism, lying, contempt, criticism, gossip, stealing, cheating, fighting, self-righteousness, abuse, neglect, abandonment, disrespect, hate, and even swearing and yelling. However, the following often-disregarded emotional states can be just as, or even more, damaging. So in this chapter, we'll explore ten ways to help you break free of these ego destroyers and use them to help you climb a ladder and shine!

1. Shame

Shame is the ego's greatest destroyer of beauty. Many of us don't even realize how deep-seated and destructive shame is to our body, mind, and spirit, and how stuck it keeps us. The ego is a sneaky thing: It loves when we're ashamed because we stay hidden in darkness, listening only to it, too humiliated to think that we could ever let our light shine.

Shame creeps up on us and fools us into thinking that we have no control over it. It can come in the guise of indifference, perfectionism, anger, control, intolerance, narrow-mindedness, and self-righteousness. It whispers into our ears that we're inadequate, flawed, or "damaged goods." It traps and convinces us that life will never get better because we aren't. Shame is the longest snake's tail, wrapping around our ankles and holding us down.

Shame has been the greatest enemy that I've personally had to release myself from. By the time I was 30 years old, I was drowning in this horrible emotion so much that I had to literally walk away from my old life, reach into the deepest recesses of my soul, and find my own inner light. Once I faced the demons of my past—from my parents' divorce to being repeatedly raped (which lead to my own teenage promiscuity) to moving out at 15 to my anger with my parents to my own divorce at 30—I really "named it, claimed it, and grieved it." I was finally able to let it go and affirm, "I am a wonderful and worthy woman. I release the chains that I have allowed to shackle me down. I am special, valuable, and beautiful!"

Letting go of the past certainly doesn't mean being in denial about it, but once we face our pasts with absolute honesty, we step into the final stage of releasing them. As Debbie Ford points out in *The Secret of the Shadow:* "Nothing can take away our life force more than the belief that we are deficient or flawed, or that at some fundamental level we are unfixable."

Shame manifests itself in the body as illness; addiction; weight problems; eating disorders; and, most always, bouts of depression. When we hold on to our pasts with shame or humiliation, we not only guarantee that we'll never move forward, but we also sentence ourselves to live in a world of constant uneasiness and self-rejection.

As Alexander Pope says so perfectly, "To err is human, to forgive divine"—and we are Divine!

Climb a Ladder

The only way to release shame is to face it—the saying "The truth will set you free" is 100 percent true. Answer the following in your journal:

- Have you done or said anything in your past that you'd never want anyone to find out about?
- Are you ashamed of something about yourself physically?
- Do you avoid people or going places because someone might recognize you?
- Are you ashamed of something that your family or spouse has done or is doing?
- Are you carrying sexual shame? (If you've been sexually abused, then you're mostly likely carrying shame.)
- How do you feel about yourself? Do you love who you are and what you've become?

Free yourself by writing down everything you've been "hiding," and then analyze it without judgment or emotion. Look at it from a soul-driven perspective—that perhaps out of a need to be loved, to survive, to comfort yourself, or because of a fear or insecurity, you made certain choices. Be honest about what part you played in it, and then let it go.

Once you've admitted to yourself that you're feeling ashamed, take the next and crucial step of sharing how you feel with someone who's nonjudgmental, completely understanding, and will never betray your trust—such as a wise friend, therapist, or support group (if you don't have one, then try ours at **www.crystalandrus.com**). While naming it is important, claiming it is the crucial step you need to take in order to grieve and release your shame. Claiming it only to yourself is usually not enough—after all, how many times have you repeated the same sad stories of your life over and over in your mind or in your diary, and have never felt any release from them? In fact, most often replaying the shame in your own mind only keeps you stuck in it. Without sharing it, you'll most likely have a difficult time ever truly letting it go.

Don't stay stuck another day, and don't let anyone convince you that you can't rise above your past. The only person who can hold you back is you! Your truth will set you free, but only if you choose to free yourself.

Daily Affirmation If You Struggle with Shame

I am worthy of love and joy and of all of life's greatest offerings. There is only the experience of this moment, and I release my past, knowing that it does not define me. I am exactly who I am meant to be. All will work out perfectly. I am worthy, special, and beautiful!

2. Pride

Pride is very devious, for on the surface, it appears to be so much higher in energy than shame or jealousy. Nevertheless, pride is still based in the ego and in its need for approval.

When most of us think of this quality, we admire it as something that can pull the poor out of their gutters, motivate individuals to do their very best work, or spur a nation to defend itself at war—yet we should never mistake the ego-driven desires of pride with those of love. Pride and love are two distinctly different things: Pride demands respect, while love never demands; pride becomes offended, while love sees beyond appearances; and love can move mountains and is the highest-calibrated emotion we can resonate at, while pride robs us of our light.

Often overlooked as justice, pride can be seen when we refuse to call a loved one over a family dispute, when we compete with others (even inadvertently), when we put ourselves deep into debt just to keep up appearances, or when we have a hard time saying "Thank you" or "I'm sorry."

I spent far too much of my earlier years immersed in this ego destroyer. I came from extremely prideful people: grandparents who'd worked their butts off to be "somebody," and parents who spent their lifetime trying to prove they were. Outside images mattered more than anything in my family. I bought my first home at 19 (who cares that I could barely pay for it!), I had shares in my first health club when I was 22, and I worked day and night to prove my worthiness. My ex-husband and I spent thousands upon thousands of dollars that we couldn't afford on our home, just to keep up with the Joneses. And I'd go for years without speaking to family members if they angered or upset me. Pride was my driver . . . and it wasn't until I walked away from my marriage with almost nothing except myself, my daughters, and my integrity—the things that mattered most—that I discovered that it's not very powerful at all!

Intolerance, narrow-mindedness, and self-righteousness all reside in the ego, and most people who live with pride aren't even aware of it because their own self-importance keeps them in denial. And since most prideful people won't ever admit to their own faults, that's why addictions are virtually impossible to overcome.

Climb a Ladder

In order to transcend, you must become aware of how entrenched you are in your own ego. Answer the following in your journal:

- Are you easily offended?
- Are you competitive—do you need to win?
- Do you get defensive when someone points out your flaws?
- Can you easily say "I'm sorry" (and really mean it)?
- Do material possessions define you?
- If your friends or colleagues were to find out that you were broke, would you be humiliated?
- Do you think that your race, religion, or nationality is superior to others'?
- Are you in a long-standing argument or estranged relationship with any family member?
- Do you have a difficult time asking for help? And if you do receive aid, do you have a hard time showing appreciation for it?
- Do you care a lot about what people think of you?

Pride actually stems from low self-esteem and a need to control. When you have to prove yourself to the outside world, you end up lowering your own sense of personal power—but by listening to your inner voice and letting it guide you, you'll discover that it's your ego that causes you to be hurt, offended, and let down. You must simply decide: Do you want to be right or do you want peace? You can't have both.

Daily Affirmation If You Struggle with Pride

Only my ego can be offended, but I am a Divine being who knows that I have nothing to prove. My soul directs my actions, and I am exactly who I am meant to be. All will work out perfectly. I am worthy, special, and beautiful!

3. Jealousy/Envy

Our ego has so many of us in anguish about how we *don't* look! That is, it has us believing that we aren't pretty enough, thin enough, tanned enough, tall enough, voluptuous enough, and so on, as we compare ourselves to other women.

The first step to claiming your beauty is to realize that you're not in competition with anyone else. The "green-eyed monster," which will destroy every relationship it touches, is one of the most damaging of all emotions. Jealousy and envy aren't indicative of love or passion—they're based in fear and are entirely about the ego. You're afraid, so you try to blame others for your feelings of inadequacy, but they're never about anyone else. Worries about how beautiful someone is or how thoughtless your mate may be stem from a deep fear that someone else is better, smarter, younger, sexier, prettier, kinder, happier, or richer (or whatever) than you are. Simply put, jealousy and envy will annihilate beauty—they cannot exist together. Until you can be truly happy for someone else's success, you'll never manifest it into your own life. And because jealousy originates from deep within you, nothing outside of you can ever alleviate it. Freedom comes once you begin recognizing the beauty that you already possess.

Also, remember that you can never make others love you or stay with you if they really don't want to. Let them go, as hard as it feels, because you're worth being loved and valued for exactly who you are. As Erin Brockovich says in her book, *Take It From Me,* when she found herself worrying about her boyfriend leaving her, she'd think, *Eric, if you can walk away from me, from our life, don't let the door hit you in the ass on the way out. If I have to go it alone, you know what? I'll still survive, I'll still make it. I like and I believe in myself, flaws and all. For every ship that sets sail, another one comes in behind it.*

On the other hand, don't force someone to continually "prove" their love to you. Neediness combined with jealousy is completely unattractive.

Climb a Ladder

If you struggle with the destructiveness of envy or jealousy, sweeping these emotions under the rug and hoping that they'll go away is never the answer. They'll eventually eat away at you and destroy any relationship that you're in. But even though you probably don't want to hold on to your negative emotions, how can you just "let it go"?

Well, the first thing to do is force yourself to do the work of uncovering your deepest fears and realize that when your jealousy rears its ugly head, it's your fear at work. So what are you most afraid of: Not being enough? Being betrayed or abandoned? Not being loved?

Each time you feel your body downshifting to this dark place, mentally talk yourself into realigning with the frequency of self-love and worthiness. When you find yourself in the middle of a perfectly wonderful day suddenly thinking about a painful experience or listening to a song on the radio that reminds you of someone who's hurt you, you need to realize that you have a "remote control" (metaphorically speaking) in your hand and you can "change the channel." You can choose to focus on what you *don't have* or what you *do.*

Realize that jealousy and envy stem from the deep-seated fear that you're not enough—and, unfortunately, no one else can ever tell you enough times that you are before you believe it yourself. Confidence can never come from outside of you . . . this is about your own feelings of worthiness. You must do the work of believing that you're enough, because *you are!* (Now in all fairness, I'm not suggesting that if you're in a relationship with someone who ogles others or obsesses over pornography that you're struggling with jealousy—but you *are* struggling with a lack of self-love.)

And finally, don't ever let someone convince you that their jealousy is a sign of adoration. Love calibrates at such a high level of energy that jealousy is obsolete.

Daily Affirmation If You Struggle with Jealousy/Envy

My life is my choice, and I choose love and compassion. I see the beauty in all things, including myself, and I know that everyone is a mirror reflection of me. I am exactly who I am meant to be. All will work out perfectly. I am worthy, special, and beautiful!

4. Procrastination

It's hard to imagine that procrastination can be this negative, but think again! We all have dreams for our lives, but when we put them off, we inevitably deny ourselves our greatest human potential. And the most important job we have as human beings is to live a purposeful life.

Those who procrastinate think that they're actually making their lives more pleasant by avoiding the tasks they don't want to do—yet each time they dodge facing a decision or getting a job done, they're actually sliding down a snake's tail and giving away their power, thus becoming a victim of their own lives.

Now, don't believe that procrastinators are only those who don't get things done. Sometimes the biggest culprits have accomplished much in their lives, yet they still avoid what they really *need* to do. Procrastinators can be the ones packing for their trip at 6 A.M. when their flight is leaving at 9 A.M.; the ones who let bills pile up, sometimes still unopened; the ones who avoid dealing with relationship issues, including commitment; and the ones who steer clear of confrontation for fear of dealing with the aftermath. Others procrastinate doing the simple (but important) household tasks that are almost effortless, yet will make life feel painful until they're done—such as tidying up, doing the dishes, organizing the cupboards, cleaning out the garage, sorting through old papers, or putting laundry away. The stress of living in a mess is so painful, yet these people will avoid doing such chores at all costs.

Some procrastinators wait until the last possible moment to get ready to go out and convince themselves that the reason they're late for everything is because they're just "so busy"! Others may forget to make doctors' appointments—going years without physicals, eye exams, or having important prescreening tests—while still others neglect to service their cars until they're forced to spend far more money when it breaks down.

Yet the most common type of procrastination comes from putting off exercising, eating well, and taking vitamins. These people are most often the ones who are "too busy being busy" to do what matters most. They just don't get around to taking care of themselves—often letting little things become the big things that get in the way of their true happiness. Procrastinators often feel as if they have the weight of the world on their shoulders and don't realize that simply making a list of what needs to be done, and then doing one thing a day, will alleviate so much unnecessary stress.

Procrastination is very different from patience. Patience is a virtue that implies faith and forbearance; procrastination, on the other hand, has nothing to do with patience, but everything to do with fear. Those who tend to put things off have a high potential for painful consequences, which can lead to feelings of guilt, inadequacy, depression, and self-doubt. For students, this can lead to dropping out and eventually a perpetual cycle of quitting tasks and becoming underachievers in life. Procrastinators can't see how much they're losing by creating drama and anxiety totally needlessly.

Procrastination is often a condition that's developed during childhood if we were taught to doubt ourselves and our ability to make the right choice. Maybe our parents had a hard time getting things done, and we simply developed bad habits by watching them—but most often it simply stems from the belief that we may fail, or we've gotten so comfortable living in chaos and disorganization that we self-sabotage even when we could easily succeed or make the situation better. Without realizing it, we give away our power and become a victim to our circumstance. Subsequently, we tend to view those who have succeeded or done the very things that we wished we could do as lucky, blessed, or maybe even manipulative, not realizing that life will only give us what we ask for . . . and it's up to us to create our destiny.

As Buddha teaches: "Effort is the root of all achievement. If one wants to get to the top of a mountain, just sitting at the foot thinking about it will not bring one there. It is by making the effort of climbing up the mountain, step by step, that eventually the summit is reached."

Climb a Ladder

Realize it's your fear that's defeating you. Procrastination is a clear sign that you don't feel worthy of living the life of your dreams. Answer the following in your journal:

- What do you procrastinate about?

- How do you think your procrastination takes you away from the present moment? What are you losing by being a procrastinator?

- What would happen to you if you were able to take the actions you needed and were successful? How would that make you feel?

- What can you do today to begin tackling the situations or projects you've been putting off? What will you gain by overcoming your procrastination?

Now take baby steps: Break down your projects or desires into small but realistically attainable goals that you can accomplish each day, and don't let yourself get overwhelmed by looking at the big picture. Then each evening before you go to bed, write down two things that you did during the day that brought you closer to living your best life and two things that you can do the next day.

You see, anxiety comes from *not* taking action. So the truth is that each time you choose to do it "now"—to make the appointment, get the job done, be more organized, deal with the problem that's looming over you, forecast and plan things out better, and so on—the instant shift in your energetic resonance will instantly elevate your illumination and beauty!

Daily Affirmation If You Struggle with Procrastination

I am motivated and inspired. Each day serves me with the opportunity to move forward and to climb ladders. I know that there is nothing I cannot do once I apply myself. I am exactly who I am meant to be. All will work out perfectly. I am worthy, special, and beautiful!

5. Regret

Sorrow, grief, anguish, woe, heartache, heartbreak . . . to endure such desolation is to live with one of the lowest-calibrating energies humanly possible. Remember that your soul has chosen every single person who's come into your life, so no relationship can ever be a mistake—not even the most painful ones. Synchronicity has brought these individuals to you for a reason.

When you regret your past, you erase the life-changing wisdom that each experience can teach you. In order for your path to unfold exactly as it should, you needed to undergo each and every one of those events to make you exactly who you are in this moment, ready to become the person you're meant to be. Letting go of the past certainly doesn't mean being in denial over the things you've done, but the bottom line is that you can't change what's already happened. Learn the lesson and move on!

Regret manifests itself in the body as illness; addiction; and almost always, bouts of depression. When you hold on to your past with sadness and loss, you not only guarantee that you'll live each day of your present powerless, but you can never move forward with excitement and passion either.

Climb a Ladder

Regret is very much like shame: You simply can't change the past, but you can begin to learn the lessons that each experience gave you.

Begin by getting comfortable. Next, close your eyes and take a few deep breaths . . . I want you to think back to an event you regret. If it was something that you wished you would have done or not done, I want you to recall that period of time in your life. Where did you live back then? Who were your friends? What job did you have?

Now think of someone wonderful you met or something fantastic that happened to you around that same year or the few years following what you regret. For example, let's say that you wish you would have gone to college, but you met a wonderful man at your job (which you wouldn't have had if you'd gone to school), and he ended up becoming your husband. And then, three years later, you gave birth to your first child. Imagine if you'd gone to college at that time—you wouldn't have your husband or your child today.

You can do this exercise with anything in your life, and you'll soon start to realize that we all make choices every day that steer our lives in a different direction. You can't change your past, so embrace it and learn from it. Let it make you a wise, wonderful woman today!

Daily Affirmation If You Struggle with Regret

The choices I made in the past brought me to exactly this moment, preparing me for the amazing journey ahead of me! I am happy with who I am and lovingly accept myself. I am exactly who I am meant to be. All will work out perfectly. I am worthy, special, and beautiful!

6. Control

Often disguising themselves as concerned, organized, or efficient, controlling people simply must be in charge, for fear that their world could fall apart. Yes, control is entirely based in fear—such individuals have been so hurt in the past that they've become too afraid to let go and allow others into their lives. They've lost their trust in others, and ultimately in themselves.

When we think that we know what's best and right, and we feel that we must exert our opinions and ways over others, we're deeply immersed in a control drama—which is the language of the ego. When we think that we have the right to tell others what to do or how to look, talk, think, or act, we diminish our own power and beauty. Issues over money, sex, and parenting—and micromanaging others—are about control . . . and the fear of losing it. Eating disorders, addictions, bossiness, jealousy, self-righteousness, obsessiveness, and possessiveness are all telltale signs of a power struggle. Sadly, controlling people hold on so tight that they end up destroying the very thing they love most.

Exerting control may give us a temporary burst of energy, but it doesn't last, and the only way to maintain it is to continue to dominate. This frequency is so dense and heavy that it puts us on a daily roller coaster of highs and lows—brief spikes of power followed by dips of anxiety or anger. As soon as we start to feel that we're losing control again, we panic and force ourselves back up, but we can't maintain this high for long.

Authentic power, on the other hand, arrives when we lose the desire to be in control . . . when we come to know and belong to that which is larger than ourselves . . . when we "let go and let

God" and embrace that life is utterly miraculous and mysterious, despite all our accumulated knowledge. We don't have all the answers, yet we know without question that all our answers will come. We don't have to be right!

Controlling people use intimidation, manipulation, and anger to silence others and get their own way. Managers, leaders, parents, and teachers who use these tactics to effect change are calibrating at such low levels of energy that they'll never be revered and honored. Control uses domination and oppression, but to instill change and inspire people—whether it's a child or a nation—we must consistently use compassion, loving guidance, soft words, patience, unswerving integrity, and dependability . . . and then surrender the rest to the Universe. This is the way to authentic power, and the only path for true change.

Climb a Ladder

Look at the following statements to see if you're struggling with control issues. Agreeing with more than five of them means that it's time for you to relax, release, and let go.

- "I'm not good at dealing with noisy or rambunctious children."
- "When I get into an argument with my spouse or lover, I can't resist bringing up old grievances."
- "When I'm under extreme stress, I become angry or irritable."
- "I have a pretty good sense of what's good for others."
- "At least once in my life I've opened someone else's mail, read their e-mail, or listened to their private phone messages."

- "I have high standards, which others sometimes mistake for criticism."

- "If it's my house, then the people in it should follow my rules."

- "I'm a better talker than listener."

- "I'm organized and efficient. I find it difficult to live with someone who's messy."

- "I rarely tell anyone that I need them."

- "I tend to be a perfectionist."

- "After a relationship breaks up, when I look back, I think that I was mostly in the right."

- "When I buy things for my loved ones, I feel as if I'm showing them how much I care for them."

- "I think that my opinions are usually pretty accurate. I'm rarely wrong, but it does happen occasionally."

- "I'll help out anyone in need, but then I feel let down when they don't think as much about me and *my* needs."

The first step is to understand how your need to be in control is affecting your relationships with others, so ask the people in your life how they feel about your tendencies. As Louis Janda, Ph.D., shares in *The Psychologist's Book of Personality Tests:* "Expect them to be reluctant about being candid; your anger is intimidating. Understand that their criticisms will elicit an intense urge on your part to justify your actions. Be calm and patient, and listen to all they have to say."

Every time you make the choice *not* to have to control, you'll realize how much nicer life is, and how much more exciting and stress free it can be when you let go of the reins. The unexpected can lead to some of life's most memorable experiences! (And trust that others have abilities and common sense, too.) Finally, do the work of rediscovering where you lost your trust and begin to redevelop your faith in your higher self.

Daily Affirmation If You Struggle with Control

I embrace my life with trust and faith. I do not always have to be right or in control. I know that there is a Divine blueprint for my life, and I am letting it unfold. All will work out perfectly. I am worthy, special, and beautiful!

7. Apathy/Blame

Apathy is a condition of helplessness, and those who live with blame suffer from the "poor-me syndrome." To be without hope is to exist in total despair, but it's our job as human beings to find purpose in our lives and to do whatever it takes to find a ladder and climb it. Once we realize that no matter where we are and what's been dealt to us—whether it's a disease, a crime, an injury, or any form of abuse—we have to find our own internal strength to rise above it. And it's here that we become truly empowered . . . after all, some of the most successful, spiritual, and kind leaders and gurus have lived through some of the most dire and painful experiences imaginable.

Apathetic individuals continually look to someone or something outside of themselves to make their lives better—while at the same time blaming that very someone or something for the reason that their life isn't they way they want it to be. Complete apathy is the state that most homeless people live in. Although many old, progressively sick, and morbidly obese individuals subsist in a similar place, just waiting for their "time to come," too many people trudge through life with this same victim mentality.

The "blame game" will keep us stuck forever. Many of us will go to our graves blaming someone else for the conditions of our lives—nevertheless, as long as we're victims, we'll continue to find ways to sabotage ourselves (most often unconsciously) in order to justify our resentment, addictions, unhappiness, and/or current failures. But once we take responsibility for our lives and release the blame, becoming totally accountable for our every action and reaction, we suddenly unleash this awesome power that enables us to overcome any challenge—whether it's to lose weight, fight an illness, quit an addiction, or get (and keep) a job we love. We respect ourselves and the world around us, realizing that although we can't control the way the wind blows, we *can* change the way we set our sails. *We're* the ones sailing this ship!

Be accountable for everything you say and do . . . *everything*. It might feel easier to blame the other guy, avoid those you may have accidentally offended, or call in sick for work because you were up late the night before—but the simple fact is that when you become totally and completely accountable for yourself and all your actions, you'll vibrate at a greatly elevated frequency. After all, accountability comes from living with integrity, and your integrity is the greatest indicator of the brilliance of your light.

Climb a Ladder

Until you change your beliefs, thoughts, and actions, you're going to continue to feel hopeless and powerless because your outer condition is reflective of your inner condition. What's so important to realize is that you co-create your experiences by creating external circumstances that mirror your internal process.

If you're spiraling downward, in a situation that you feel totally victimized in or know that isn't your fault, and you don't know how to take back your power, answer the following in your journal:

- Why would you co-create this? What are you gaining by staying stuck?

- How do you use your blame as an excuse to stop you from doing what you really want in life?
- What are you really afraid of?
- What are you losing by blaming others and keeping yourself stuck?
- How would releasing blame and letting go of your "story" improve your life?

You may have had some truly terrible assaults in your life—be they emotional, mental, or physical—but if you're carrying around the low-calibrating energy of blame, you're only attracting more negativity back to you . . . and *you're* the one keeping yourself stuck now.

You do have the power to rise above any condition that you're living with, but before any change can occur, you must first realign your energy back to your former childlike love, joy, and unconditional forgiveness. You must then understand that each experience was something that your soul chose in order to learn and evolve (believe it or not!).

Daily Affirmation If You Struggle with Apathy/Blame

I create my life through my thoughts and actions, and they are positive and powerful. I know that the Universe wants only the best for me and that nothing is a mistake. I have all the power I need tucked deep inside of me. I am exactly who I am meant to be and all will work out perfectly. I am worthy, special, and beautiful!

8. Resentment

Resentment is one of the worst burdens that holds you captive in life. An emotion of the ego, if left to fester, this bitterness kills you slowly . . . body, mind, and soul. The ironic thing about resentment is that it only destroys the person who's doing the resenting. Like acid on a Styrofoam plate, eventually it burns a hole deep inside you. If you carry resentment, you'll never be able to retain your energy—you'll never be transcendentally beautiful.

Feeling resentful of someone who's caused you pain is a common reaction, but the only way you can move forward is to forgive those who have hurt you, be they stranger or friend. Sure, that can take a little time, especially if the wound is new, but refusing to find forgiveness is refusing your own beauty and power. Now this doesn't mean that you wipe the slate clean or sweep what happened under the carpet and move on—it means completely releasing *the resentment.*

Many people simply won't forgive . . . they can't allow themselves to. They truly believe that their pain is too deep to let go of. Others say that they forgive, but they can't forget. Well, both sentiments will end up eating them up inside.

It's natural to feel upset, especially when you've been hurt or abused, but in order to move on to more beautiful days and make new wonderful memories, you must realize that you have to let it go.

Climb a Ladder

If you're not creating everything that you want in your life, you're probably holding on to resentment toward someone. In other words, you're still more committed to your "story"—to being right—than to your success and happiness. Yet as I said in *Simply . . . Woman!* releasing resentment is very much like facing your fears: It actually appears much harder than it really is.

Visualize anyone who's hurt you in your mind's eye. See him or her standing in front of you and say out loud, "I forgive you, ________________ [say their name]." Say it over and over until you lose the emotional charge. It may take 10 times; it may take 100; but eventually, you'll feel the anger dissipating in you. See this person as a scared and hurting individual who only lashed out because of the messages of his or her own ego.

Every time you start drifting back to negative memories, stop yourself and say out loud (even just to yourself), "I forgive you, ________________ [say their name]." It might not feel authentic—it may even seem futile right now—and that's okay. Your thoughts will begin to change your beliefs . . . which will then affect your actions . . . which, in turn, will transform your outcome. Living with transcendent beauty will become effortless!

Daily Affirmation If You Struggle with Resentment

Letting go means letting God. Just as I want to be forgiven for my trespasses, I forgive all those who have hurt me. I love all life, and I only desire peace and joy. My intentions are for peace. All will work out perfectly. I am worthy, special, and beautiful!

9. Guilt

Guilt is different from shame: Shame says, "I'm bad"; while guilt says, "What *I did* was bad." You see, guilty people are always worried about breaking their own moral code, and they feel guilty if they engage in some behavior that they don't believe to be proper. Many who struggle with guilt also allow others to blame them for their unhappiness—using a victimlike unconscious control maneuver, they begin to make choices to please others, even at the sake of their own personal integrity or justice.

When we convince ourselves that we merit condemnation or blame, we fall prey to the low-calibrating emotion of guilt. When we negate our own voice—our own truth—in order to please someone else or to ease our own feelings of guilt, we instantly slide down a snake's tail, lose light, and give away our power.

One of the biggest things I've had to learn was that I'd made so many choices—from keeping staff that I should have fired to splitting money on projects that I'd done 99 percent of the work on to staying in relationships that weren't good for me—just to ease my own guilt. I didn't want anyone to be mad at me or think I was like Nellie Oleson, so in order to make myself feel better, I gave away my personal power and often my integrity. In the end, I always felt low and resentful. *Ah, the sleepless nights!* Subconsciously, I thought that as long as I was taking care of everyone else's needs, I'd be loved and admired . . . but that never happened. You see, we teach people how to treat us, and unless we're treating ourselves with dignity and respect, no one else will either.

A huge part of claiming our beauty comes from claiming our *lives,* even if it means that someone gets upset with us. I've only recently learned that abiding by our souls doesn't mean having peace at all costs, even at the sake of our own personal needs and integrity. Having personal *power* is different from personal *integrity.*

Understand that unless we're highly calibrated, we human beings will lash out like terrified animals when we're afraid. Most of us will try to use guilt to make ourselves feel bad so that we give in and give up. We then resign ourselves to a life of resentment . . . we become martyrs.

It doesn't matter how far we've come in our journey of self-discovery; it takes daily effort to create an inner dialogue that's unshakable, undeniable, and limitless. Soul-driven people have trained their minds in the same way athletes train their bodies—to conquer their fears and feel confidence, joy, and inner peace. This mental training begins by deciding that they're going to stop reacting to others' dramas and emotions and stay strong for their own integrity.

Climb a Ladder

If you've hurt someone, then you need to apologize, but staying stuck, feeling bad, and wishing you could do it differently can't (and won't) change the situation. You'll never rise above your past as long as you feel guilty for what you've done, especially by trying to ease your conscience by giving away your own power.

If you have patterns that need to be changed—that is, you continually create situations in which you inevitably let others down—you need to determine why. But choosing to continue to self-punish and deny your personal power is counterproductive.

Ask yourself: "What am I losing by always feeling guilty about taking care of myself? And what am I gaining by not?" You may surprise yourself with your answers, since most guilty people have actually fallen into the unconscious control maneuver of the victim.

We must all stand on our own two feet because we're never responsible for someone else's feelings. When others blame us for their disappointment or anger, we must compassionately understand where it stems from, but we can't take it on as our own issue. Sufism says that there are no mistakes in life, only lessons. When we feel ashamed about our choices or our pasts, we deny ourselves the life-changing wisdom that each experience can teach us.

Daily Affirmation If You Struggle with Guilt

No one can make me feel anything unless I choose it. I speak my truth and abide by my soul, even if others try to convince me that my actions are otherwise. I am exactly who I am meant to be. All will work out perfectly. I am worthy, special, and beautiful!

10. Fear

Everything comes down to fear and love: Each choice we make is either ego driven or soul driven. Fear is what holds us back in life—it finds every reason why something won't work, why we aren't loved, why our dreams are silly, and why we're destined to fail. Fear is the permissive undercurrent in our society, for it is the cause of anxiety, addictions, self-righteousness, racism, gossip, betrayal, anger, and violence.

Fear immobilizes us and makes us lazy, self-sabotaging, and guilt ridden. It makes us jealous and shameful and creates pride and procrastination. Fear is the cause of control, and it has millions of us running to our doctors every year in search of a magic pill . . . often by the name of Prozac or Paxil. And although it's natural and smart to have a healthy fear of situations such as jumping off a building or walking into a dangerous neighborhood, many of us allow fear to dictate the majority of our choices.

Facing your fears is much easier than it appears—in fact, Susan Jeffers writes about it eloquently in her best-selling book *Feel the Fear and Do It Anyway!*

Climb a Ladder

Each time you find yourself making a decision from a stance of "But what if?" catch yourself and instead ask, "But what if I don't?" Do a quick mental inventory by answering the following:

- What's the worst thing that could happen if you do this (within logical and reasonable boundaries)?
- Could you deal with that outcome?
- What's the best thing that could happen if you do this?
- How would that make you feel?
- Would it be worth taking the risk?

Fear is the principal cause of regret, since it's the things you *don't* do in life that you regret most: You didn't pick up the phone and make that call to create peace in a relationship for fear that the other person would snub you. You didn't go to the bank to get that business loan for fear that they'd say no. You didn't pursue the man of your dreams for fear that he'd reject you. You stayed in an abusive relationship for fear of being alone. You fear, you fear, you fear . . . and in doing so, you keep yourself stuck.

Once you realize that you'll be okay no matter what comes your way and that God will never give you more than you can handle, you can begin to live in a state of courage and faith. Your beauty will radiate, and people will be magnetically attracted to your strength!

Daily Affirmation If You Struggle with Fear

The Lord is my shepherd, I shall not want. He maketh me lie down in green pastures: he leadeth me beside the still waters. He restoreth my soul: he leadeth me on the path of righteousness for his name's sake. Yea, thou I walk through the valley of the shadow of death, I will fear no evil: For thou art with me: Thy rod and thy staff they comfort me. Thou preparest a table before me in the presence of mine enemies: thou annointest my head with oil; my cup runneth over. Surely goodness and mercy will follow me for all the days of my life and I will dwell in the house of the Lord for ever.

— Psalm 23

We come into this life with only a soul.
There is no body. There is no mind.
We leave this life with only a soul.
There is no body. There is no mind.
Beauty is in the soul.
— Crystal Andrus

Chapter Seven

Absolute Energy Equals Absolute Beauty

One week before finishing this book, I gave a talk for my alma mater's alumni banquet. When I first arrived, a beautiful blonde instantly approached me. She had an effervescent smile, and she illuminated the entire room. There was just something about her, and I knew that we were meant to connect again. Within minutes, we were exchanging e-mail addresses.

Toward the end of my speech—during which I spoke about our relationship with our parents and how our emotions play themselves out through our bodies—I noticed this woman intently listening. Her arms were gently wrapped around her body and tears were streaming down her face, and I intuitively knew that she had a powerful tale to tell. And boy, oh boy, did she ever! It was a story that I knew needed to be shared, so here it is in her own words (which have been edited for clarity).

Shere's Story

On April 22, 1953, I came into the world feetfirst, kicking and screaming, about a month early. They say that I was deformed and bruised at birth and certainly nothing much to look at. They called me Shirley (after Shirley Temple), but when I left home at 15, I changed my name to Shere.

I don't remember much of my childhood—in fact, it's almost a blank until age 13. Most of what I know about myself has come from stories told to me by neighbors and family members. I do remember my parents saying that I was "ugly, stupid, and a slut." I remember being beaten repeatedly. I remember believing myself to be such a horrible creature that I deserved to be beaten. Of course my parents were also struggling—financially and with each other.

From age 13 to 15, I kept running away from home. Not far . . . but away from the house. When I was 15, the school stepped in and had me taken out and put into a foster home. I remember leaving with a suitcase of clothes—no toys or books or keepsakes. There were no tears or good-bye hugs . . . I just moved out and barely saw my family (including two sisters and a brother) until 1971, when I married my first husband at age 18.

He enjoyed drinking and hitting . . . and I found myself running away once more, looking for any kind of love—in all the wrong places. Within two years, my husband and I were separated, and I again found myself out on the street with my clothes, a few dishes, and some ratty pieces of furniture.

From age 20 to 23, I went from man to man looking for love and security. I didn't find it. But I did find more abusive and controlling men. Only now, as I look back, do I realize how desperate I must have been.

I met my second husband in 1976. He was ten years older, and an extremely generous man. With his two small children, ages four and nine, I was finally going to have the love and family I never had. My new husband adored me and wanted to take care of me, so we moved away to start fresh.

Since I didn't have children of my own—and I wasn't sure if I ever wanted them (afraid of my own "damaged blood")—I found being a stepmom very difficult. I resented my husband's kids and any attention they received from him. Eventually, I found myself feeling insecure again, so I began the search for someone else's "undivided attention." It was the '80s, and the nightclubs were filled with promise. . . . My marriage ended soon after.

Then I met Jeff. He was 10 years younger and 50 years wiser than I was. We dated off and on for seven years, and he was so patient and devoted. I had a hard time committing myself totally to him—and then one day, he said that he'd had enough with me and was gone. It was at that moment that I became an adult. It was only then that I realized what I'd lost. Up until that point, I truly thought that I was having so much fun making up for all the lost years that I didn't see it coming.

Months went by, and the pain never went away. My love for Jeff grew stronger, and eventually we found our way back to each other and have never looked back. We've been married 15 years, and our love is one that people write books about.

Somewhere in all this, my ego had begun to run rampant. At age 15, I weighed 200 pounds, thanks to my first job working in a bakery. I found comfort in that warm, loving bread. For my first wedding, I lost the weight, but following the first divorce, I gained it all back and then some—I tipped the scales at 220 pounds. My second husband, being the loving and encouraging "father" that he was, introduced me to the game of squash and enrolled me in classes to help me build my self-confidence. I lost the weight and gained plenty of confidence. Well . . . at least it sort of felt like confidence.

I joined a talent agency and did modeling in print work and commercials, and I finally got a regular show as a TV host. I was totally focused on being so beautiful that no man could resist me—not even the delivery guy. I believed that I was the ugly duckling who had turned into the beautiful swan . . . and I could write a book about all the men I seduced over the years.

Then in 1997, I received a rude awakening when I lost my job. Jeff and I had just purchased a large home, and we had no idea how we were going to pay for it. That same year my father died, and as sad as it was, his death opened up a treasure trove of suppressed emotions. All the "should haves" and "could haves," along with all the fights and the pain, came flooding back in waves. My mother had already died in 1986 and I thought that I'd put that part of my life behind me—but I hadn't.

I was suddenly out of work and feeling so afraid and lost. Waking up every day with no place to go brought forth feelings of failure and reawakened the buried pain of "stupid." For about a year I moped about in our brand-new, much-too-large house and felt sorry for myself. My health wasn't great, and I was seeing a chiropractor two to three times a week for pain, PMS, and headaches. My visits to the doctor were also frequent, as I complained of stomach pain, constipation, and myriad problems relating to digestion, only to find out that I had irritable bowel syndrome (IBS), as well as an ulcer, a hiatal hernia, and endometriosis!

My chiropractor and I became close—after all, I saw more of him than anyone else. One day he presented the idea that I should start thinking about what was causing all my health challenges and think more about prevention—that I should take control of my wellness.

At first I didn't take him seriously because I thought that I knew better. But he eventually got through to me, and I started taking some natural supplements to help balance and build my hormones. Within four months, I was completely free from the ailments of PMS (pain, depression, anxiety, and bloating), which was major for me. This was also the turning point when I started to think outside the box, making my own decisions and taking charge of my life.

For three years, I lived and breathed the "wellness in body, mind, and spirit" philosophy. I attended every lecture, read all the books, subscribed to the health magazines, started working in a health-food store, and began studying about glycobiology and glyconutrients. I was guided to learn meditation and practice yoga, and I sought out new healing modalities—iridology, Reiki, acupuncture, and music therapy. I saw medical doctors who were open to holistic therapies and experienced all the new tests: saliva tests, inner-terrain tests, blood tests, you name it—I tried it all. I figured that since I was happily married, I'd now have to settle for being just the "health goddess."

And then in 2000, my soul woke me up.

A mammogram, x-ray, and dreaded biopsy revealed that I had cancer in my right breast. How could this be happening to someone who'd just spent the last three years doing everything she could to get well, stay well, and prevent any sickness?

The next few months were terrifying. The first surgeon I went to had absolutely no sympathy for me, and his bedside manner left a lot to be desired. I went to see his partner in the same office, and their dispositions were like night and day. He was a young man of Asian descent, with an open mind to alternative therapies. His message, however, was the same: I'd have to undergo surgery followed by chemotherapy and possibly radiation. The difference was that he explained the procedure and the possible side effects, and he encouraged me to continue taking alternative therapies if my belief was that strong.

My husband and I left this doctor's office feeling calmer than we had in weeks. Now it was time to do some soul-searching. I researched and read everything I could about breast cancer. I gathered information from my friends at the health-food store, as well as my nutritionist. I talked to my husband, family members, and close friends. I chatted with the doctors at Mannatech (the research-and-development company that discovered the science of glyconutritionals). And last, but most important, I talked things over with myself.

I concluded that the operation and side effects were worse than the disease itself, and even if the disease was removed from my body, the chances of it coming back were high because I hadn't yet determined or faced the reasons why I had the gift of cancer in my breast in the first place. So until I knew the reasons, why put my body through the trauma?

My wellness focus changed. Although I had to take care of myself physically—I stopped drinking coffee, soda, and alcohol completely; I ate organic whenever available; I didn't use a dishwasher or microwave; I stopped wearing perfume or toxic nail polish; and I decided to choose a very holistic lifestyle, including natural makeup and cleaning products, purified water, lots of supplements and greens, and an intense regimen of glyconutrients—my focus was now on understanding why the cancer had manifested in my breast.

This took me on a journey that surprised even me. One day during a walk, I spotted a beautiful, soft, grassy area, and I sat down and closed my eyes. I suddenly saw myself surrounded by shimmering bookcases, filled with volumes as far up and as out as my eyes could see. I could read the names of the books, and I could touch them and pull them off the shelves. The library was harmonious with nature, and there were gardens and trees mingled throughout. I saw my precious cats who had passed on, and they were happily chasing birds and butterflies through the lush green forest.

I continued to walk into the vastness of this library, and I came across a woman. I barely recognized her at first, and then I realized that it was my mother. She hugged me and said, "Hello, dear. We've been thinking about you," and in that instant, my father appeared. They both looked radiant and translucent. My dad told me that he missed me and his love for me was never ending . . . and I immediately understood the depth of his love. I began to cry as I implicitly realized why, in his life as my father, he'd abused me and driven me away. I knew that he truly loved me and that we'd both agreed to reincarnate as father and daughter in this lifetime to learn the lessons that our souls both desperately needed in order to evolve.

*In that instant, I forgave myself and them. I felt more love than ever before, and I was sobbing uncontrollably by now. They both hugged me and said that it was time for me to leave the library and return home. Before they left, I asked them what book I should read, and they said, "*How to Know God* by Deepak Chopra."*

Then they were gone, and just as quickly, the shimmering books and gardens faded away. I was left sitting on the grass, crying. But something had changed in me—I was suddenly lighter and felt released . . . I felt childlike. I knew I was loved. I, Shere Donald, was loved!

It was clear to me now why there was cancer in my breast. You see, the breasts are the center of love and nurturing, which I'd searched my whole life for—not just from my parents or siblings, but from the world. And until that moment, I hadn't known just how much the Universe loved me . . . how much it loved everyone. Now that I'd found nurturing and love, my breast could heal—my heart *could heal.*

I went for a routine test not long after and was told that there was no longer any cancer in my breast. I was beautiful—every part of me was.

I don't "claim" breast cancer or any other disease now. It no longer defines me or grows within me. With forgiveness and love, I've released it from my body, and all tests confirm that there is no cancer regrowth.

What I do know is that wellness is a journey, and I'll always have to stay focused on it to stay well. I must be consciously aware of my humanity, while still turning over the pages of my life's book. And every now and again, a past pain will surface to gently remind me that love will conquer all as long as I allow it to.

Get in the Flow

This chapter is designed to take you on a journey—a very deep and metaphysical one—in which you'll travel far within your body and access the central source of your beauty.

Don't panic if it seems as if I'm speaking a foreign language or it's too "way out there." When I first started to discern that most of my aliments were really just healing opportunities that my soul was showing me via my body, I was a little skeptical, too. But now that I'm free of the pain of a once-excruciating monthly ovulation and awful PMS; cervical spine problems that took me to orthopedic surgeons, physiotherapy, and massage therapy for years; and an ongoing struggle with my weight and moods, I now wholeheartedly believe that our bodies are merely messengers, and once our inner self flows freely, the outside can take care of itself. This is our "knowingness."

What most people don't realize is that our genetics only account for about 10 to 15 percent of our ailments. The rest comes from what we do to ourselves—what we eat, drink, breathe, speak, and think, as well as how we process our emotions. Even with all our technology, information, counseling, psychiatry, and prescriptions, most of us still can't figure out why one day we feel great and the next we feel doomed. Nor do we know why we attract certain people and then repel them soon after.

I believe that most human problems—be they mental, emotional, physical, or spiritual—are caused because we can't align our personalities with our souls. Therefore, we have an inability to resonate with the highest universal frequency of beautiful bliss and to radiate it freely within our bodies.

All of this takes an integrative approach: If we're not supporting our physical bodies with the proper nutrients, no amount of emotional work will stabilize us. If we're praying and meditating but not moving or exercising, we may still feel tired and sluggish. If we're eating well but aren't being who we really are, we'll still ache with an inner emptiness. This combined approach of strengthening the body, breaking down mental and emotional roadblocks, and allowing the soul to be revealed is what I call "Integrative Body-Mind-Soul Healing."

Once we listen closely, we can understand exactly what's going on beneath the surface. It's then that we can *heal* our pain—not bandage it. Once we get aligned energetically, our energy will rise, fear will become obsolete, and we'll become the "I am." We'll transcend and flow with a breathtaking and immensely powerful beauty.

Doing this physical/emotional energy work is very much like peeling back the layers of an onion. Just like Shere Donald, who unabashedly told her truths, once you name it, then you can claim it . . . and then you can grieve it, release it, and detach from it. It will no longer own you.

Throughout this book, I've taken you on a slow and gentle journey, beginning with your earliest years, your relationship with your parents, and your view of yourself, and then on to the rest of the people in your life, including other family members, friends, lovers, and co-workers. Each one of these individuals has had an effect on your life. When your body is in perfect alignment with your mind, you're able to effortlessly process all the worldly information and messages that you've received with detachment and love. But you *are* human, and although your quest is for enlightenment—to transcend the ego and to live with Divine grace at all times, where you are love and love is you—you'll still have times when you feel hurt or offended. The messages get skewed, and you become disconnected from your higher self.

When I begin working with a client, I start with a body assessment. Although emotions don't originate in the physical body, they do produce chemical reactions within it. Looking first at recurring injuries, illnesses, symptoms, and muscle imbalances, I then balance clients' systems physically, first focusing on nutrition and exercise . . . making their temples strong! Then, using both intuition *and* logic, I ask them to describe where and how they feel the emotional link may be playing itself out, and I allow myself to feel what I think is happening with them. Based on what I've discovered, I then explain how this emotional/physical correlation relates to different parts of their lives—or their "consciousness." Then we really get to work!

The Seven Energy Systems

You can practice what I do for my clients for yourself. Trust in your intuition, listen to your body, and be honest about your truths, fears, and feelings. Only you can change you! Remember that each emotion you feel—from concern over your safety and feelings of self-respect and personal power to your ability to trust and love, stand up for yourself, be wise and compassionate, be open to other's ideas, and know that you belong to that of the greater good—all falls into one of seven energy systems in the body called *chakras.*

CHAKRA CHART

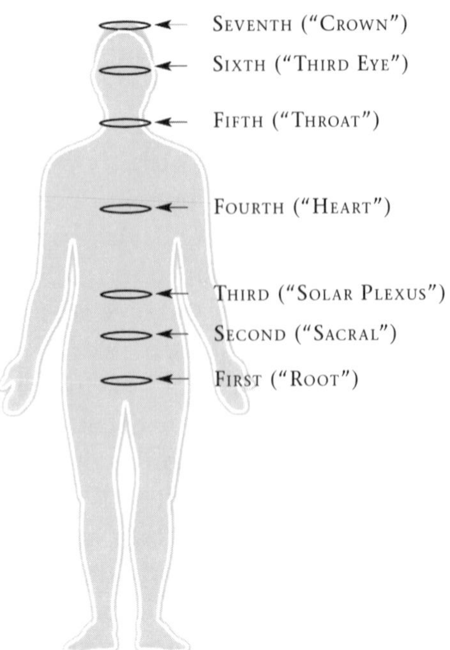

Chakra is a Sanskrit word meaning "wheel" or "vortex." The seven chakras are like sensors that run along your spine, connecting your "physical self" to your "intellectual self" via your "emotional self." Each one processes different energies (from those around you, as well as universal energy) and creates different emotions—along with symptoms within your body if blocked.

A Balanced Body

In an ideal world (that is, one in which we're raised with fearless and loving parents and we trust in ourselves and in life), our energy would flow perfectly throughout our systems. It would begin in our childhoods, where we'd be raised in a safe and loyal environment. Our maternal bonds would be deeply established by being breast-fed and nurtured by our mothers, with our fathers close by, ready to lend a helping hand.

Our parents would be strong role models in our lives, as we'd spend plenty of time with *both* of them, knowing that we were always safe and provided for. And we'd most likely have a large extended family filled with loving aunts, uncles, cousins, and grandparents. Our emotional, physical, and intellectual needs would always be met, and our roots would be strong and stable. By the time we were five years old, we'd feel as if we belonged to someone or something greater than ourselves. As this grounded and secure feeling developed, our **first chakra** would flow freely.

As we grew, we'd develop a strong body as we ate wholesome foods and took our vitamins and essential fats. We'd run and jump, moving our bodies with confidence and ease. As we entered into puberty, we'd develop healthy beliefs about our bodies and sexuality. Strong boundaries would be set, although we'd still have a natural innocence and curiosity. As our bodies matured, we'd begin to embrace our sexuality with a natural comfort. We'd like who we were and would look forward to falling in love.

We'd see our parents playfully kidding around with each other, kissing and hugging, and as we became young adults, our creative juices would flow freely—we'd write, paint, sing, and dance. We'd trust in our passion, knowing that we'd always be able to provide for ourselves, just as our parents had provided for us. There would be no money issues in our homes, and the bills would be paid without a fight. We'd trust that money, love, and security would always flow with abundance into our lives. Our energy would continue to flow up through our **second chakra** and into our third.

As we grew into young adults, we'd trust in the world, knowing that it would never fail us and that *we* could never fail either. As we listened to our gut instinct, we'd never doubt ourselves or worry about our ability to succeed. We'd like ourselves and innately know that the world did, too. We'd have plenty of friends who'd never let us down, and we'd feel an immense sense of personal power. We could be or do anything—we'd feel unstoppable! As our bodies developed, we'd feel physically strong, full of vitality and confidence. We'd eat rich bioenergetic foods, and our hormones would be perfectly balanced. Our **third chakra** would flow freely as it entered our fourth energy system.

As we developed into women, we'd embrace love with a pure and open heart. Although we'd know that things wouldn't always go our way, we'd realize that love was our right and would effortlessly attract many soul supporters. We'd love and easily nurture ourselves and others. We'd forgive easily and be able to express all our emotions—including frustration and anger—in a healthy and productive way, knowing that we'd still be loved even if we sometimes got upset. We'd innately understand that love can heal anything and that holding on to resentment would only hurt ourselves. We wouldn't have any enemies and would know that pride was poisonous. Our **fourth chakra** would sparkle as we felt a profound love for all things, including all people, plants, animals, art, and music. We'd love the skin we were in and would continue to honor ourselves with healthy food, loving movement, and conscious breathing.

Finally ready to embark on our life's path, we'd feel confident and free to speak our mind, follow our hearts, and always live with honesty and truth. Lies would never be an option, and we'd know that although it could be tough at times to stand up for ourselves, we'd always abide by our own personal integrity—we'd become candles in the wind and pillars of strength. We'd share our gifts effortlessly with the world, as we refused to listen to our mind-made selves. Our **fifth chakra** would shine with an intoxicating glow.

With our fifth chakra activated, we'd move effortlessly into the **sixth chakra,** where intuition, synchronicities, and mental acuity would become a normal part of our daily existence. We'd process our emotions by abiding by our higher selves and manifesting miracles with the power of our thoughts. Our bodies would be healthy and agile, while our minds would be vibrant and inspired. We'd embrace life with utter faith and logic.

As we entered into our **seventh chakra,** the endless source of omnipotent and absolute energy would pour endlessly into this opened "crown chakra" and flow down through all our other energy systems. We'd know that we were connected to the Divine and that we *were* the Divine. As we transcended beauty, time would become obsolete. We'd become the "I am."

Unfortunately, few of us were raised in an ideal world by fearless parents. Instead, we've dealt with our challenges—our emotions and fears—in whatever way we learned how. Trust in the world has been scattered, and we've worried that people might see us for who we really were . . . flaws and all. Subsequently, we've become what we believed we were, right down to the cellular level. Our energy has become blocked; and we've probably begun to notice ailments, illnesses, fears, and anxiety taking over.

Having said that, it *is* possible for us to go through our lives completely free of disease and physical illness, even if we were abused, neglected, or betrayed as children. It isn't the abuse, neglect, or betrayal that makes us ill—it's the way our bodies process and hold on to such acts.

The Soul Revealed

Think of the energy flowing through your system like water in a stream. When everything is moving freely without blockages, you feel healthy, as your cells resonate with pure positive energy. However, when one or more of the chakras are blocked (this is an unconscious thing until you become aware of these energy systems within your body), the emotional energy gets stuck and begins to back up. Debris and toxins begin forming, and your body starts to shut down. The blockage is caused when your mind-made self takes over from your higher self and processes the energy.

The ego whispers negativity into your cells, and your body starts to show signs of illness, depression, fatigue, and weight gain. You can't figure out why yesterday you felt great, but today *nothing* makes sense. You begin to notice aches and pains, and you find yourself with recurring injuries or illnesses.

Yet when you tame the beast by choosing to process your emotions through your higher self, your chakras become balanced and your body becomes one with your soul . . . you're aligned. Once this happens, you're able to experience the world in a way that appears almost magical to other people. Synchronicities direct your life, and you resonate at the highest vibration possible. Your beauty is beyond all comprehension, and everyone who meets you is intoxicated in your presence.

Healing the Chakras

There are many ways for you to assess your inner energy system and do your own Integrative Body-Mind-Soul Healing, but first you must determine which chakra(s) may be blocked in your body.

Begin by saying a prayer to your Higher Power, such as: "I ask you to guide me through your gift of spirit. Open up my eyes and show me what it is that I need to heal." Then quietly think about your "weak link," or the area that continually takes a beating when you're under extreme pressure. Do you suffer from pain in your neck or lower back, or do you get a cold sore? Are you easily constipated when under stressful situations? Do you get migraines, or are you more likely to develop an ulcer? Does your throat tighten up when someone yells at you or does your stomach churn? Does your heart begin to palpitate or do your shoulders clench? All of these physical symptoms are easy identifiers.

Another way to discover touchy areas of your body is to look at a recent photo of yourself: Do you seem comfortable and at ease, or are you nervous and apprehensive? What does the photo tell you about yourself or the physical areas that you may be holding pain in?

The most effective way to determine your hidden blockages is by doing a guided meditation. By simply getting comfortable and taking a journey in your mind's eye, you can see where your blockages are radiating from. That is, you can intuitively feel what's going on within.

Sit down somewhere comfortable, and with your eyes closed, imagine that you're scanning your body with a specialized machine that can look either on the surface of your skin or deep within.

First ("Root") Chakra

Begin at your feet, ankles, calves, and knees. Do you feel or see any pain (think of recurring injuries, arthritis, or varicose veins)? Move up into your thighs and bottom: Do you have sciatica (pain along the course of your sciatic nerve, especially in the back of the thigh)? Have you had tumors or fissures in your colon or rectum?

I also want you to think about your immune system: Is it taxed and tired or serene and strong? Are you depressed or struggling with your moods? Chronic fatigue, fibromyalgia, chemical imbalances, spinal problems, blood disorders, and other immune-related diseases are also characteristics of an imbalanced first chakra; and obesity is now being linked to a block in this area as well. All of these symptoms stem from the inability to manage the emotions that are associated with your earliest years—with your family of origin.

This first energy system is called your "root chakra," and it's symbolized by the color red. This is where family wounds are stored in the body, and key words surrounding it are *safety, security,* and *belonging.* This energy system can become unbalanced or blocked if you felt afraid as a child, perhaps abandoned by a parent through neglect, abuse, divorce, or death. It can also be imbalanced when it's too open—that is, when you've been totally smothered by one or both of your parents and don't feel independent and able to stand on your own two feet.

Although this chakra is linked to childhood, it can also be shattered if you lose a parent unexpectedly or experience long-term separation or abandonment from your family at any age—you're alone and afraid, and don't feel as if you belong. Blockages can also be related to "family scars" and the life script given to you by your parents and grandparents. If you carry shame passed down through the generations, then it's highly likely that you suffer from symptoms of a blocked first chakra.

Most often, though, those who suffer from an imbalanced first chakra are those who don't feel as if they have someone that they can always depend on. Perhaps they had parents who worked too much or who neglected them because of addictions or depression.

I always think of those with a balanced root chakra as being like a mighty oak tree, virtually impossible to knock down—whereas someone with an imbalance in this area is like a little flower with tiny roots, which can be plucked out and tossed away with little effort.

Answer the following in your journal:

- Do you feel safe and secure in your life?
- Do you feel grounded and stable?
- Could you always count on your mom and dad? If not, do you have a hard time letting people get close to you?
- Are you close to your extended family now? Were you close while growing up?
- Do you have a large circle of friends or people whom you can count on?
- Do you really not concern yourself with what people think of you?

If you've answered no to one or more of these questions, then you may benefit from some work on your first chakra (see page 204).

Second ("Sacral") Chakra

Now let's move on up into your pelvic area, uterus, ovaries, and bladder—what do you envision in your mind's eye? Do you see any ob-gyn problems or any sexual dysfunction? Do you have difficulties with menstruation, PMS, pregnancy, ovulation, or childbirth? Do you suffer from hormonal imbalances, or do you experience the hot flashes and depression of menopause? Do you have bladder problems, endometriosis, fibroids, or cervical dysfunction? Do you have a low sex drive, or the opposite—an insatiable appetite? Do you have hip problems or lower back pain, or have you had appendicitis? Are you jealous and possessive?

This all relates to your second, or "sacral," chakra. Symbolized by the color orange, it relates to your relationships and is also your center for creativity. It's where your need for other people, as well as your desire to control things in your external life, comes from. An open and flowing chakra is seen when you're able to set healthy and well-defined boundaries and then trust in them. Money, sex, and relationship problems are rarely about what you think they are—instead, they most often are a power struggle due to your *fear of losing control.*

This chakra often becomes blocked if you've experienced domination by rape, but can also happen when you feel oppressed by addictions, betrayal, abandonment, or poverty. (I've also seen blockages in women who've had abortions or extramarital affairs and haven't released their shame or properly dealt with their past experiences.) You often abuse or medicate yourself by engaging in meaningless sex with many different partners or shutting down completely and becoming abstinent. When you're afraid, you can't let go, so you hold on to whatever tiny bit of control you feel you still have in your life. You use guilt, blame, or shame in your relationships and have difficulty communicating your truest needs. And you may become obsessive-compulsive, a perfectionist, or a workaholic.

Answer the following in your journal:

- Do you embrace your femininity and sexuality without judgment?
- Do you still have an innocence and wonder about sex and love?
- Do you make love in the soul of sex?
- Do you carry guilt or shame about having an abortion or an affair, or from being abused?
- Did your parents handle money well and instill a respect of it into you?
- Are you fine with other people knowing things about yourself or your family, even if they're embarrassing?
- Can you let people see you without your masks?

If you've answered no to one or more of these questions, then you may benefit from some work on your second chakra (see page 206).

Third ("Solar Plexus" or "Navel") Chakra

Let's continue up into your intestines, bladder, appendix, stomach, liver, gallbladder, kidneys, adrenal glands, and middle back. Do you see inflamed organs or beautiful energy flowing through and around them? And do you suffer from indigestion, ulcers, colitis, or irritable bowel syndrome?

These all relate to your third, or "solar plexus" or "navel," chakra, which is linked to your feelings of competence and adequacy in the world. When you feel balanced, you believe in yourself but don't define yourself by your external accomplishments. You strive to be your best, but don't need approval from others. This chakra is where you get your gut feelings; and it represents your personal power, ability to trust, and level of confidence and self-esteem. Shown as the color yellow, its key words are *instincts, power,* and *action.*

Answer the following in your journal:

- Do you struggle with maintaining long-term committed relationships?
- Do you routinely get indigestion, heartburn, ulcers, hernias, or adrenal problems?
- Do you suffer from diabetes or pancreatitis, depression, weight gain, or eating disorders; or do you struggle with addictions?
- Are you possessive and territorial, or do you trust people?
- Do you fear criticism, rejection, or looking foolish?
- Are you afraid of getting old or fat?
- Do you tend to let your mind-made self take over—that is, does it seem as if your ego is always talking?
- Can you be both overly sensitive and aggressive, depending on the situation and your perception of threat?

If you've answered yes to one or more of these questions, then you may benefit from some work on your third chakra (see page 209).

Fourth ("Heart") Chakra

Heading up to your chest area, look at your lungs: Is the air flowing through them, sending massive amounts of oxygen to your heart and other organs, or is it shutting down, panting for energy? Do you suffer from problems such as asthma, bronchitis, or pneumonia? How about your heart—do you have coronary artery disease, hypertension, chest pain, or valve problems? What about your upper back and shoulders—are they tight and stiff or relaxed? How are your arms, wrists, and hands (think of recurring injuries)? And finally, have you had cysts, fibroids, or cancer in your breasts?

This area relates to your fourth, or "heart," chakra (which many say is the "seat of the soul"). Shown as the color green, its key words are *healing, kindness,* and *empathy,* and it represents the balance of emotions and your ability to express them in a healthy way. If you can give and receive love, forgive and forget, show compassion, and unconditional acceptance of others, and let go of hostility and grief, then this chakra is nice and balanced for you.

However, if this energy center is blocked, you probably feel weighed down with anger, despair, hatred, or even envy. Yet the heart chakra is not about the outside world—of what people have done to you—but rather, what you're now doing to *yourself* because of it.

Answer the following in your journal:

- Have you had your heart broken?
- Are you holding on to past pains and resentment?
- Do you feel as if you're carrying the weight of the world on your shoulders, or are you holding any grudges?
- Do you find it difficult to give easily and effortlessly, without any expectation in return?
- When you give your love, is it conditional and fearful?
- Do you feel unworthy of being loved, or is it hard for you to receive love as well as give it?

- When you feel as if a "hurt" is coming, do you become cold and distant, shutting people off easily?

If you've answered yes to one or more of these questions, then you may benefit from some work on your fourth chakra (see page 211).

Fifth ("Throat") Chakra

Continue your mental focus up toward your neck: Is it stiff or free of tension? How about your throat, mouth, lips, teeth, and tongue? What about your ears and jaw? Do you have thyroid or cervical disc problems? Do you get canker or cold sores when you're run-down? This all relates to your fifth, or "throat," chakra, which represents communication, integrity, and personal will. Shown as the color blue, it rules the throat, neck, and shoulders. Key words are *truth, honesty,* and *self-expression.*

If this energy center is blocked, you may experience sore throats, painful or swollen glands, head colds, a stiff neck, or struggle with drug, cigarette, or alcohol addictions. Yet once the throat chakra is awakened, you'll become fearless. Once fear is obsolete, the "I am" can emerge as you freely express yourself in all situations. It's the fear of not being accepted for your truth that causes you to lie. But the biggest lie you can live is denying yourself your personal integrity. "Your truth *will* set you free. . . ."

Answer the following in your journal:

- Do you tend to deny your own personal truth and refrain from speaking your mind?

- Are you ignoring your dreams?

- Do you have a hard time saying what you really need or want? Do you find that you don't even know what your needs or desires are?

- Are you unable to detach from outcomes and abide by your soul?

- Do you tell people what you think they want to hear instead of your most honest thoughts and opinions (although always with diplomacy and tact)?

- Do you avoid confrontation, even at the cost of your own personal justice?

- Do you have a difficult time saying no? Or do you speak before you think, respond too hastily, or talk over others, never listening to their points of view?

If you've answered yes to one or more of these questions, then you may benefit from some work on your fifth chakra (see page 213).

Sixth ("Third Eye") Chakra

Moving into your head, look at your eyes, brow, and forehead: Are you frowning and stressed or relaxed and at ease? Are your pineal and pituitary glands pumping out "happy endorphins," or are they tired and drained? Do you suffer from headaches, visual problems, nightmares, earaches, or insomnia?

This relates to your sixth, or "third eye," chakra, which represents intuition, along with mental and reasoning abilities. Shown as the color purple, its key words are *imagination, openness,* and *wisdom.* Once your third eye is awakened, you'll begin to intuitively know your life's purpose, and you'll effortlessly enjoy the journey.

Answer the following in your journal:

- Can you let yourself seek counsel in the wisdom of others?

- Are you fearless about looking within and discovering your deepest truths?

- Can you logically separate your perception of reality from others' viewpoints?

- Can you release the old and embrace the new, or take the path of least resistance?

- Do you abide by the philosophy of "live and let live," refraining from judging others?

- Can you accept that you don't know everything and that others can also teach you? Are you flexible in your thinking?

- Are synchronicities and miracles commonplace in your life?

If you've answered no to one or more of these questions, then you may benefit from some work on your sixth chakra (see page 215).

Seventh ("Crown") Chakra

Finally, think about your entire skeletal system and all your muscles—your framework, so to speak—do you feel strong, fit, and nourished, or do you see an ailing body that's falling apart? How about your skin—does it glow, or do you struggle with acne, psoriasis, or eczema?

This all relates to your seventh, or "crown," chakra, the highest one on the body and where you merge with the Divine! This energy system symbolizes mystical connection, devotion, and spirituality, and key words are *enlightenment, being,* and *human awareness.* Shown as the color white, the crown chakra represents the total alignment of the mind, body, and spirit.

When this chakra is balanced, you're at one with the world and open to receiving the Divine Universal Collective Energy. You've become the "I am," and your higher self is revealed. It's here that energy flows effortlessly through the body, and you embrace life with a magical ease. Miracles become commonplace and worry obsolete.

When this chakra is blocked, however, you lose faith in the Divine and essentially the entire meaning of life. You feel spiritually abandoned, or even worse—you reject the entire notion of a mystical realm. You lose touch with your higher self and abide only by the ego.

Answer the following in your journal:

- Do you pray? Do you believe that your prayers are answered?
- Do you trust in a Divine blueprint for your life, never questioning that everything will work out?
- Are you afraid of the afterlife?
- Do you abide by your Higher Power?

If you've answered no to one or more of these questions, then you may benefit from some work on your seventh chakra (see page 217).

Prayer Is Potent

About two years ago, I was in a hotel room about 2,500 miles from home, getting ready for the biggest seminar I'd ever given. I'd been up since about 5 A.M., meditating, doing yoga, and praying. I needed every bit of power and strength I could acquire . . . and yet I still felt so afraid and unsure. *This seminar,* I thought, *could make or break my career.* As the last hour ticked by before I was to leave my room, I got down on my knees, lifted my arms to the sky, and looked up. I begged God not to let my words fail me as I walked onstage later that day.

In that moment, I experienced something that would forever change my life. I had a complete surrendering, wherein an overwhelming knowingness overtook my entire being. I'd prayed all my life, but this was different. I was suddenly filled with an exhilarating energy that, at the same time, gave me absolute calmness and peace. I instantly knew that my words would never fail me, for they weren't *my* words. I began to overflow with tears and was completely taken over by a euphoric feeling of bliss.

I walked out on that stage as a new woman. I was no longer trying—*I'd become.* And I knew it.

I realize now that it doesn't matter if you've only known this feeling for a day or for a thousand years, once you know it—you know it. And you can never lose that awareness . . . that precious gift of knowingness, confidence, contentment, and surrender . . . where your heart spills over with love and your fears are obsolete.

For weeks afterward, everyone who entered my presence told me that I looked more beautiful than they'd ever seen me. I knew what it was from!

Prayer is one of the most powerful ways to transcend beauty, protect your light, manifest miracles, and connect with the Divine Universal Collective Energy. But just like all thoughts, it must have a positive intent, with the unwavering gratefulness and belief that your prayer has already been answered. When you pray with gratitude, you essentially acknowledge that you implicitly trust that all will be as it's meant to be.

As Neale Donald Walsch says in his thought-provoking book *Conversations with God:* "You will not have that for which you ask, nor can you have anything you want. This is because your very request is a statement of lack, and your saying you want a thing only works to produce that precise experience—wanting—in your reality."

I personally have an almost never-ending dialogue with God: I chat with Him as I run, while I drive, or anytime I feel unsure or afraid. Simply knowing that He will never forsake me gives me an innate sense of power (perhaps from the knowing that I'm a part of Him and He is a part of me). This dialogue is the constant reminder that I'm never alone and that as long I stay "checked in," all my needs and questions will be answered.

In the wonderful little book *Your Needs Met,* Jack and Cornelia Addington have created "spiritual mind treatments," or scientific prayers that we can use and apply in our own lives. Since an individual thought process can redirect our harmful thinking patterns, these prayers put our mind in total alignment with our higher self. (You certainly don't need someone else's prayers to connect to the God within you, but if affirming prayer isn't something you've ever done before, then I highly recommend a book like this.) The very first prayer is one for attracting abundance, and its simple yet profound message captured me: "There is no lack but lack of faith in God. . . . The will of God in me is Wealth, not want, but I must not hinder the will of God by belief in lack, or by telling God how my good shall come to me."

The undisputed power and protection of prayer can even be documented scientifically. In the most widely publicized study of this, cardiologist Randolph Byrd studied 393 patients who had been admitted to the coronary-care unit (CCU) at San Francisco General Hospital. Byrd's study was to observe the therapeutic effects of praying to a Judeo-Christian God, and to evaluate the effects of prayer in a CCU population, a prospective randomized double-blind protocol was followed.

Over ten months, 393 patients admitted to the CCU were randomly placed into one of two groups: (1) the prayer group (192 patients), where Christians outside of the hospital prayed for them, and (2) the control group (consisting of the remaining 201 patients) who weren't prayed for. Neither the patients nor the hospital staff knew which group they were in. The results, while surprisingly wonderful, didn't surprise those who prayed: The consistent and overwhelming data suggested that prayer has a beneficial therapeutic effect, because those being prayed for had far fewer cases of congestive heart failure, cardiopulmonary arrests, and pneumonia. They also needed less ventilator assistance, antibiotics, and diuretics.

Another astounding study was one in which a survey of 131 controlled experiments found that prayed-for rye grass grew taller, prayed-for yeast resisted the toxic effects of cyanide, and prayed-for test-tube bacteria grew faster.

No matter what your religious beliefs are, *I* pray that you embrace your God with appreciation and gratitude, knowing that your prayers will be answered.

Amen!

Just Be

Taking the information that you've just gathered from this chapter, let's practice the Integrative Body-Mind-Soul Healing and balance your inner energy system. Let's get you into the flow!

When understanding your chakras, it helps to think of the bottom three as interrelated and the top three as interrelated. When your root chakra is blocked, for example, you'll grapple with control and trust, and if you've been sexually abused, of course you'll naturally struggle with feelings of safety and security. The first three chakras are the lower aspects of your consciousness (safety, control, and personal power), the top three are the higher aspects of your consciousness (integrity, intuition, and spirituality), and the heart chakra is the bridge that connects them.

Once you've identified which chakra(s) are blocked, you must begin to make sense of the emotional baggage you're still carrying. To do so, you need to think back over your life and identify where the energy flow became blocked. You then need to name it, claim it, grieve it, and release it—once you do, you'll feel your physical symptoms lifting, and you'll be brighter, lighter, and transcendentaly beautiful!

An important aspect of your healing is truly letting yourself be healed. I see so many people who can't let go of a past pain, so they're continually in a "state of healing." They won't let themselves *become* because they're always *trying*.

This may be risky for me to say, especially since I believe 100 percent in 12-step programs, but I find it sad that people who haven't had a drink in 20 years still call themselves "alcoholics." I understand and support their feelings of being "powerless to alcohol" and that they should never drink again . . . but it's the label they carry for life that concerns me. If you were a prostitute when you were 18, does it mean that you're one for life? These are shame labels, which so many of us hold on to without realizing that when we do, we keep ourselves stuck. I think that naming and claiming your past is essential, but then once you've grieved and released it, it's time to let go of your label, too. You are not your disease, your addiction, your medicine, your occupation, your name, your country, your race, or your religion. You are not your circumstances.

Don't commit yourself to an aspect of your personality either. For example, you're not "irresponsible" or "lazy" just because you may have been that way at one time in your life. You're not "unstable" or "neurotic" because you may have acted that way before. You're not "sleazy" or "unworthy" because once upon a time you may have been sexually promiscuous. And you're not "dysfunctional" because your family wasn't "normal" by society's standards. If you do occasionally fall back into self-punishing behaviors, realize that it's often your setbacks that can catapult you forward with massive power. So claim your healing!

Live as though you're healed, and refuse to give power to it when you occasionally backslide into a "familiar" feeling. Just like downshifting in a manual transmission can actually gain you some speed, you must sometimes slow down, pull back, and regroup in order to fly forward and climb a ladder. Don't assume that all perceived setbacks are actually setting you back. You can often look back and see that some of the toughest times were, in fact, periods of your greatest growth.

Now let's get started!

The First Chakra

If your roots aren't strong, the rest of your life will feel weak. Just like an oak tree, you must give yourself strong roots, even if you didn't develop them in your childhood. It's time to take the steps to heal the past. . . .

1. Look back at your childhood and write out your earliest memories in your journal. What learned messages did you adopt? What beliefs did you take on? What is your life script now?

2. After you've named it, you need to claim it. By sharing your pain and fears with someone else, you'll give validation to what you've

gone through. Sharing your family "secrets" isn't a betrayal—until you face them, and then share them with someone trustworthy and nonjudgmental, you'll never heal them. Look into finding a great therapist or life coach who can bring you through this. Remember that shame says, "I am no good," while guilt says, "What *I did* was no good." Nothing about you is a mistake, and releasing shame is mandatory if you are to shine in all your glory. (*Healing the Shame That Binds You* by John Bradshaw can also be a powerful tool for letting go.)

3. Join a local support group, for which there should be many listings in your local telephone directory. Or please join ours at **www.crystalandrus.com**—our online journal is also an incredible place for healing and self-discovery.

4. Learn more about your mother, grandmothers, and great-grandmothers. Discover the meaning of their lives to understand how they've affected yours. The river runs deep, but once you make peace with your past, you'll flourish in your future!

5. Do you really know your father? If not, learn more about him and his childhood. Begin by looking at the world through his eyes, which will give you more insight to who *you* are. Remember that you can only heal that which you're willing to face!

6. List all the blessings that you received from your family. Focus on the positive contributions of each member.

7. Take omega-3 essential fatty acids *daily!* This is not an option—it's mandatory—for it will help with depression, stabilizing your moods, and improving countless other conditions.

8. Get all the exercise you can. Running, aerobics, dancing, or walking are great ways to feel grounded, while yoga or Pilates are ideal practices for getting centered and restoring balance.

9. Hire a personal trainer to help repair any muscle imbalances in your body. Do resistance training to build an inner sense of stability.

10. Connect with Mother Earth: Walk on the grass barefoot, spend time in nature, and visualize yourself firmly planting your feet on the ground.

11. Visit your family. Take the time to talk on the telephone and use e-mail only for business—it's become a terrible wall between human connections.

12. Create a new one if your family of origin has passed on or is too toxic to spend time with. Make an effort with aunts or uncles, cousins, or grandparents.

13. You need to be around other people, so get involved in outside activities. Join a club, gym, or organization; and organize dinner parties or barbeques.

14. Eat red food—strawberries, cherries, raspberries, tomatoes, papaya, watermelon, and so on. Have warm baths with red salts. Wear red clothes. Paint your bedroom or office (or wherever you spend the most amount of time) red.

15. If you have children, give them roots and wings. Never deny them the opportunity to know your parents and siblings. And never hold them back out of your own fears of losing them.

The Second Chakra

When you feel oppressed or out of control, you often hold on even tighter. However, when this chakra is blocked, your power mutates into force, and you become manipulative and controlling. You feel afraid, and therefore, you attract more fear into your life. (Remember the law of attraction: You attract what you emit.) Until you balance this energy center, you'll continue to attract relationships that bring about pain and/or you'll never feel as if you have enough money or love, regardless of your bank-account balance or mate. It's time to take the steps to let go. . . .

1. Start by reactivating your creativity by painting, singing, drawing, or writing. This energy will draw you into a dialogue with your ego, and you'll then begin to release your fear and pain.

2. Begin writing daily in a journal. Notice how your fear of losing control is holding you back in life. (I also offer an online personal journal, where no one needs to know your name, which gives you an outlet to reveal your secrets and release your shame. Go to **www.crystalandrus.com** and click on "Message Forum.")

3. Discover your innate beliefs about love, sex, money, and relationships—then compare them with your logical views and see if they match. If not, burn your old beliefs and recite daily affirmations that reestablish your new perceptions of reality.

4. Pick out your favorite tunes and blast them in your living room. Dance without any restriction for five minutes every day for a month. Let the music come alive in your body . . . reawaken your sensuality.

5. Release control by reciting the Serenity Prayer daily:

God grant me the serenity to accept the things I cannot change,
Courage to change the things I can,
And the wisdom to know the difference.

6. If you've been abused—sexually, verbally, or physically—professional help is often necessary to restore balance here. Find a good therapist, counselor, soul coach, priest, or pastor. Share your shame, and then once you name it, it's time to claim it. From there, you can begin to grieve and release it.

7. Dare to walk naked. Go without makeup for one month (okay . . . do it for a week). Don't wear it to work, out to dinner, or to visit with friends—only put on moisturizer and sunscreen. Note how others will treat you the same if you carry yourself the same way without cosmetics. You have to know your own beauty in order for the world to see it.

8. Ditch your strict schedule for a week and try living life embracing the unexpected.

9. Taste foods and drinks you've never tried. Be adventurous—eat delicacies from around the world, including India, Japan, Bulgaria, the Caribbean, Germany, Italy, China, France, Thailand, Greece, Portugal, Ireland, Scotland, and Mexico.

10. Take a hot bath, light candles, and arouse your natural sexual energy. Learn to love all your parts!

11. Choose to make love without masks. Stay in the soul of sex, and be at ease.

12. Honor yourself when you put on makeup by doing it with gentleness and care. Celebrate your reflection without worry or wishing.

13. Notice the beauty in other women, too! Refuse to gossip or be envious of others. Each time you bite your tongue, you elevate your own personal power—and soon the fears will leave you permanently.

14. Wear orange, eat orange foods, bathe in orange bath salts, and paint your bedroom or office (or whatever room you spend the most amount of time in) orange. Close your eyes and visualize a healing orange light moving through, and around, this chakra.

15. If you can't seem to let go of your trust and control issues, and you believe that they may be causing physical as well as

emotional problems, start by reading more about the body-mind-soul connection. Books such as Louise Hay's *You Can Heal Your Life* and Dr. Christiane Northrup's *Women's Bodies, Women's Wisdom* are wonderful places to start.

The Third Chakra

Raising your self-esteem is only possible if you take back your personal power. Remember that power is very different from force because it's not about manipulation or control. It's about trusting in yourself—being the very best "you" possible—and then relinquishing the need for approval. It's about knowing that you alone are enough . . . and that you're worthy of all of life's greatest offerings. It's time to take the steps to be the woman you're meant to be. . . .

1. Write out your life story (script). This may seem narcissistic, but it's incredibly empowering.

2. As you read over your life script, pay attention to where you began to lose your voice. Notice the ways in which you gave your power away, even if you were a child. What have you lost by your experiences? And what have you gained?

3. What can you do today to begin taking back your power? Think of three things, even small ones, and commit to doing one of them before the week's end.

4. Learn to love the skin you're in! Stop buying beauty and fitness magazines that try to convince you that you're broken—*you're not.* Look in the mirror at least once a day and say, "I love you. You are beautiful."

5. Become accountable—that is, say what you mean and mean what you say. If you've given people your word, then don't let them down.

6. Get physical. Exercises such as martial arts, boxing, kick-boxing, and weight lifting will give you a sense of power and strength. And do lots of abdominal and lower-back exercises—after all, your core is the center of your powerhouse!

7. Eat a rich bioenergetic diet, but watch overeating. In other words, listen to your gut without feeding it. Also, don't forget to drink plenty of water and take your supplements. And consider taking one digestive enzyme with each meal.

8. Wear clothes that let you breathe. Get rid of the control-top pantyhose or girdles—let your own strong stomach muscles be your support!

9. Choose a great naturopath and be tested for allergies (especially to gluten). Be open to alternative medicines.

10. Believe people when they give you their word—to feel trust, you must give it.

11. Change the channel when you feel yourself downshifting and giving your power away.

12. Surround yourself with positive people and identify energy drainers (your gut will warn you when you're around one of them!).

13. Wear yellow, bathe with yellow bath salts, paint a room yellow, and place yellow flowers on your desk at work. Close your eyes and visualize a healing yellow light moving through, and around, this chakra.

14. If you're struggling with claiming your power and purpose, please make the additional effort of really making peace with it. Cognitive therapy, spirit coaching, and even self-help books such as Rick Warren's *The Purpose-Driven Life* and Dr. Wayne Dyer's *The Power of Intention* are wonderful places to start.

15. If you're too bossy or defensive on the surface, yet suffer from feelings of inadequacy and self-doubt, use the trick for catching on fire: Stop, drop, and roll. Of course I don't mean that you should literally do this, but before you respond to someone with a hasty rebuttal or become defensive when you feel as though somebody's let you down, *stop*—bite your tongue. Then *drop*—drop out of the conversation for a minute, take a deep breath, and relax. And then *roll*—most often, nothing is ever as bad as it seems, so let the small stuff roll off your back!

Here's another helpful saying: "When in doubt, don't." That is, always give yourself a few days to process something you're unsure of. Analyze it to be certain that you're truly abiding by your higher self. I live by the three-day waiting rule: If I'm really upset about something, I'll make myself wait three days before I respond, return an e-mail, or call someone back. I'm sorry if they don't like it, but I must be accountable for my actions, and I need to be sure that it isn't my offended little ego that's lashing out.

So let go of your need to be right. It serves no one . . . especially you!

The Fourth Chakra

This chakra is far more evolved consciously than your first three energy centers. It's where you can take all of your life's experiences and transform them from pain into lessons. Here, you let go and let God, and you release your need to be right. By now you should have named it, claimed it, and grieved it—so it's time to take the steps to release it. . . .

1. Find forgiveness. Let go of past pains no matter how justified you think they are, and remember that love can heal anything. Each time a past pain gets triggered, say out loud: "I release this. I am no longer angry. Love will heal this." Then never bring it up again . . . ever. Pride and resentment are such damaging and life-draining emotions that are based purely in the ego. Let go and let God.

2. This also means learning to really love yourself. Keep in mind that you get what you give, but you can't give what you don't have! When you deny aspects of yourself, you'll just search them out in others—so learning to love *all of you* is totally necessary so that you don't project your issues onto the people in your life. One of the best books I've ever read to help face and accept ourselves is Debbie Ford's *The Dark Side of the Light Chasers*. Pick up a copy or listen to Debbie on her radio show on **HayHouseRadio.com**™ to uncover your own shadow.

3. Commit yourself to healing all the relationships in your life. Before spending time with your loved ones, decide that you'll have peace . . . no matter what! Watch how they begin to treat you differently, too.

4. Take up swimming or yoga and do upper-body stretching—exercises that expand your chest, stretch out your shoulders, and open up your lungs.

5. Be kind to everyone—without exception—including animals and plants. Spend time outside, surrounded by greenery. Look strangers in the eyes as you pass them by, smile, and say "Hello."

6. Do the Mirror Exercise from Chapter 4. Look at your reflection with loving eyes and see the beauty that's already within you. Read your list of beautiful things about yourself at least once a day—preferably three times daily!

7. Before you go to bed each night, note five things that you have to be grateful for in your life.

8. Become aware of your breathing—it will help with all problems in the heart chakra. Set time aside every day for "conscious breathing."

9. Every time you feel afraid, notice how your shoulders contract and remind yourself that your heart is contracting, too. Open up

and expand your lungs, and drop your shoulders. Visualize green light flowing through, and around, this chakra.

10. Volunteer—give to others for nothing in return!

11. Choose to align your energy with the universal frequency of love. Each time you feel a lower-calibrated emotion taking over, remind yourself of a time when you felt the overwhelming power of love and adopt that feeling. *You must choose love!* Soon it will become effortless to live this way.

12. Eat green foods, wear jade and green clothes, surround yourself with real plants and flowers, and paint your bedroom or office (or the room you spend the most amount of time in) green.

13. Hug your children. Pet your dog. Kiss your grandma. Get a massage or give one. Touch your lover. Human contact is essential... feel the magical energy it brings.

14. Be patient and compassionate. Remember Jesus' words as he hung on the cross: "Forgive them, for they know not what they do."

15. Let yourself receive love. You're only as strong as the people around you, and constantly being the pillar, the fixer, the giver, or the lover will eventually drain you dry.

The Fifth Chakra

Here, you enter into higher consciousness. You've released your worries about the world and now must take your natural place in it, remembering that there's a distinction between personal power and personal integrity. It's time to take the steps to give meaning to your life. . . .

1. Never lie, under any circumstance. Speak your truth, even if it's scares you, for it builds your character and empowers you.

2. Live your "truest truths." Look at your life and all the choices you've made up to now, and ask yourself if they were to please others, to look good, or out of fear. Are you happy living this way anymore? What actions can you take to get back your life and abide by your truths?

3. Set your own personal boundaries. If you have something on your mind, say it with love and diplomacy, but *say it.* The alternative is a loss of personal integrity (and many sleepless nights!).

4. Listen to beautiful music, including chakra-balancing CDs such as Colette Baron-Reid's *Journey Through the Chakras,* Steven Halpern's *Chakra Suite,* or Robert Aviles's *Sanctuary.*

5. Talk less and listen more. We have two ears and one mouth for a reason.

6. Fight fairly—don't yell, but please don't be silent either. Communication is the art of negotiation.

7. Follow your life's path and never sell out. Just as in the movie *Field of Dreams,* if you build it, they will come. You don't necessarily have to quit your present job today, but start manifesting the one you want. Hire a life coach to help get your career/life on track if you're really struggling with finding your way.

8. When you're feeling unsure, confused, upset, or angry, write out your thoughts and feelings in a journal. Make sense of your emotions before you "spout off at the mouth" and say something that you can never take back.

9. Learn to say no graciously.

10. Tell your partner who you really are and who you once were, and trust that he or she will love you no matter what. Your

truth is your freedom! (And remember that those who truly love you will deal with whatever you share.)

11. Manifest miracles. Use visualization to see yourself where or how you want to be—with your eyes closed, imagine how you'll feel as this miracle takes place. Keep in mind that sickness originates in the mind before it ever gets to the body.

12. Find a great chiropractor who will align your spine and release the reservoirs of negative energy stored within your body.

13. Wear blue, bathe in blue bath salts, and paint your bedroom or office (or the room you spend the most amount of time in) blue.

14. Close your eyes and visualize a healing blue light moving through, and around, this chakra.

15. To silence the unremitting babble of the ego, stay engaged: Each time your mind starts to wander off—worrying, wondering, planning, and speculating—bring it back to the present. Stay aware of the present moment. Eckhart Tolle has a brilliant book called *The Power of Now,* which is one the most compelling works for teaching us how to transcend the ego and embrace the Divine within each of us.

The Sixth Chakra

This chakra is where you separate your perceptions of the world, of yourself, of life, and of others, and you allow an unbiased, nonjudgmental expression to direct your thinking. When you're balanced, you've silenced the ego and are abiding by your soul. It's time to take the steps to realize that all is well in your life. . . .

1. Redefine your interpretation of your life's experiences with logic and wisdom. Use your intellectual self, rather than your mind-made self, to process your emotions.

2. Keep in mind that meditation and visualization are helpful in balancing this energy center. Close your eyes and focus on envisioning your third eye directly between your brows. Once you're focused, you may see it, but it could be closed—be sure to stay focused on it until you see it opening. Your third eye is the window to the Other Side.

3. Focus on intentions, rather than outcome. Things can't and won't always go your way.

4. Discard self-righteousness. Attract soul supporters without labeling them and expecting them to be who you want them to be. Allow people to climb their own ladders while you climb yours.

5. Recognize which self you're serving—are you answering to your mind-made self or your higher self?

6. Keep your atmosphere as energized as possible. Learn about feng shui, which is the art of placement within a home to increase energy and flow. A fantastic book to get you started is Denise Linn's *Sacred Space.*

7. Limit your use on a cell phone (even the earpiece isn't protective enough), and sit back at least three feet from your computer monitor. If you're using a laptop, get a separate keyboard.

8. Let go of petty worries and fears and trust in the Divine blueprint for your life.

9. Abide by your synchronicities: The Universe will continue to send you the people, places, and events necessary for your evolvution. Intuition is the thread that connects you to your higher self—trust it!

10. Be a candle in the wind, and use temptation to climb your own ladders.

11. Wear purple, put purple flowers on your desk or around your home, bathe in purple bath salts, and paint your bedroom or office (or wherever you spend the most amount of time) purple.

12. Discover simplicity—most of your life is filled with distractions that take you from the Divine Collective Universal Energy.

13. Keep visualizing your body being in harmony and sending beautiful healthy messages to every single one of your 100 trillion cells.

14. Close your eyes and visualize a healing purple light moving through, and around, this chakra.

15. Activate intuition by eliminating all toxins in your life and by reading wonderfully insightful books such as Sonia Choquette's *Trust Your Vibes* or Colette Baron-Reid's *Remembering the Future.* Align your personality with your soul!

The Seventh Chakra

When this chakra is balanced, you know that *you've arrived.* You've come home! Fear is surrendered, and you're at peace with yourself and all others. It's time to take the steps to reveal your soul and live an absolutely Divine life. . . .

1. Visualize your crown chakra opening up and receiving the Divine Collective Universal Energy.

2. Pray for your family, community, and Mother Earth.

3. Have a craniosacral massage, or try another form of energy-aligning bodywork such as Reiki, Reconnective Therapy, or the like.

4. Close your eyes and visualize a healing white light moving through, and around, this chakra.

5. When in doubt, don't. Turn it over to God and release it, knowing that the right answer will come. Have patience.

6. Remember that you can't always make sense of why something isn't going your way, but have faith and trust that there are great powers at work that can see many years down the road.

7. Place religious icons, crosses, statues, or meaningful spiritual artifacts in your home or office.

8. Find a spiritual community that works for you—whether it's with a traditional religion or New Age church, the message should embrace love, light, and unity and make you feel enlightened and alive!

9. Claim your spiritual gifts, but remember that you *never* have to prove your enlightenment to anyone.

10. Embrace your mortality. Life is eternal, and there is nothing to fear.

11. Invest in Doreen Virtue's *Goddess Guidance Oracle Cards*. Each day, spread the cards across your heart and pick one—they're not only really fun, they truly seem to evoke the goddess in each of us!

12. Take the path of least resistance . . . go with the flow and adapt to the situation. When your body and mind reject what's happening, relax rather than resist.

13. Wear white, and paint your bedroom or office (or whatever room you spend the most amount of time in) white.

14. Turn off your TV, light a candle and some incense, and relax with a good book. Some of my favorites are *The Celestine*

Prophecy by James Redfield, *Siddhartha* by Hermann Hesse, *The Seat of the Soul* by Gary Zukav, and the Holy Bible.

15. *Transcend beauty. . . .*

Afterword

Your Rite of Passage

We've come to the end of this journey, and now it's time to cross over. It's just like looking from the outside of a beautiful sanctuary—from behind huge iron gates and into the perfect garden—and then finally gathering up the courage to open the doors and step through them. To be in the garden, realizing that it was created for you . . . only you can give yourself this gift! And the moment that you relax, rejoice, and release, you'll know that you've arrived.

This is your rite of passage, and when it happens, you must claim it! You must walk it, talk it, and know it, in every cell of your being. Sure, tough days will come again, for that's the rhythm of life, but once you honor *you*—your beauty, passion, purpose, truth, fears, and voice—you'll know that all is as it's meant to be and that *you* are exactly who you should be.

Start creating rituals for yourself. Make a list of things that you wish your "knight in shining armor" would do for you, and then start doing them for yourself. Tell yourself every day that you're beautiful. Buy yourself fresh flowers for your bathroom, your office, and your kitchen. Run yourself hot bubble baths and surround your tub with candles. Play soft, soothing music and cook yourself fabulous dinners, using your best china. Wear great outfits that make you feel great, even if you're not going out. Honor your body with massages, facials, or pedicures. And nourish yourself with foods that will love you back. In other words, begin treating yourself like the queen you are!

If you struggle with this notion, then it's time that you redefine your interpretation of what a queen is. I believe that she's honest, gentle, wise, kind, strong, just, fair, and fun. She's authoritative, accepting, charitable, noble, confident, courageous, ethical, and beautiful. She's truthful, virtuous, leading, and liberating. She knows what she wants and isn't afraid to go after it. She has a humble confidence and a gentle strength, and she makes no apology for who she is. She is woman, in all that it encompasses. She is *you!* So envision this queen and put on your "crown," for it is time for you to take your rightful place in the world.

When each of us claims our life and the right to be ourselves—beautiful in all our glory—the entire Universe falls into alignment. Human consciousness evolves, and the world becomes heavenly.

You are beautiful . . . so be it.

Acknowledgments

To George Katsikis, my lover, best friend, and lifelong companion—you've taught me more about love and the magic it bestows than I truly believed was possible. Your presence in my life has been so visible in my outer world, but the changes in my inner world have been even greater. I love you!

To Madelaine and Julia Dantas, my beautiful little girls—you both have such gentleness, grace, and gusto that will inspire the world. All I can say is, "Shine, babies, shine!"

To Donna Andrus, my mother—you are intensity, intelligence, and intrigue, all wrapped up in one beautiful blonde bundle! Thank you for allowing me to share such personal parts of our lives so openly and generously. We've finally found each other, and I love you so much! It's your time to fly!

To Ed Andrus, my dad—we've all traveled a tough and narrow road, but it has brought us to greener pastures, lovely wildflowers, and vibrant sunsets. I love you for your strength, tenacity, charisma, and diplomacy. You are my daddy . . . always and forever.

To Marion Raymer, my maternal grandmother—without you and your loving guidance, I wouldn't be who I am . . . I wouldn't have my mother or my daughters . . . I wouldn't have my own life. Thank you for your strength and courage. You are transcendently beautiful!

To Tiffany Andrus-Robertson, my baby sister—you've risen above so many insurmountable challenges to become such a magnificent woman, mother, and wife. Follow your dreams and continue to *shine!*

To Jeff Andrus, my big brother—you're a man of strength, integrity, and family values. I humbly respect you and all that you've accomplished. You taught me more about focus than anyone in my life. Thank you.

To Edson Andrus IV, my little brother—you are more than you know, and I love you, little guy! Keep your head to the stars!

To Tracey Andrus and Mike Robertson (and Abby, Emily, Mason, and Spencer)—my brother and sister selected such beautiful people to grow old with. Take good care of them and all my precious nieces and nephews.

To Alice and Edson Andrus, my paternal grandparents—I love my "Andrus blood," and I love the gift of confidence and dignity that you've bestowed on us all.

To Lambros and Julia Katsikis, my father and mother in-law—you've embraced me and my girls with such love and kindness. You're what "good people" are made of! I thank you for raising such a beautiful son.

To Maria and John Pedias—take care of your precious family, and be well. Much love!

To Colette Baron-Reid, an extraordinary singer, songwriter, author, and international intuitive counselor—you're not only my soul sister, but through your powerful gift of spirit, you've honored me in a way that no other woman ever has. I admire and respect you—what a shining star you are!

To Mary Kim Harper, my greatest supporter—you're always on the sidelines, ready and waiting. Thank you for all that you *are* and all that you *do*. You're truly an amazing woman, and I send you my deepest love forever and always!

To Jill Kramer, editorial director at Hay House—thank you for all that you do and for making Hay House feel like home.

To Shannon Littrell, my editor at Hay House—thank you for really "getting me" and embracing this book the way you so lovingly did. You're the best! Truly . . .

To Amy Gingery, my art designer at Hay House—thank you for taking my vision and creating a masterpiece. Bravo!

To Annette Doose and Catherine Lisa, my "true blues"—imagine . . . 20 years of friendship, and never a moment of doubt! Part of both of you lies inside of me . . .

To Renate Cunneen—your growth and healing is a true testament to the power of God. You're finally shining with all the magnificence I always knew was within you. And I know that you'll continue to be a light in this world.

To Margot Boccia—you're not only one of Hollywood's most sought-after makeup artists, you're also a stunningly beautiful woman, on the inside and out! Thank you for believing in this book from day one and for reinforcing it every time we spoke.

To Kamen and Julie Nicolov at KD Studio Group—thank you for such a great Website, logos, e-mailers, and newsletters, and for always believing in and supporting me. *You are family!*

To Sam Graci—you're the kindest, gentlest, most exuberant man I've ever known. You make me a better person just by being in your presence!

To Stewart Brown—you've believed in and supported me in such a significant way that you unknowingly gave me strength when I sometimes thought that I might fall. I appreciate everything you and Genuine Health have done for me.

To Lisa Chisholm, Tara Stubensey, Alan Logan, Letelle LeClair, Aurea Dempsey, Naomi Kolesnikoff, Joe Graci, David Cole, Steve Thompson, Nora Fromme, Nicole Wall, Sheena Dufour, Gordon Newell, Phil Oudin, Janice Partington, Ophelia Loy, Nathalie Simard, Lisa Kilgour, and the entire team at Genuine Health—your unbelievable support and constant encouragement has gone miles beyond my expectations. You're an intricate part of my success, and I thank you!

To Michael Webb—your generosity and support have been tremendous. You're a man of unbelievable integrity and patience, and the world needs more men like you!

To Beth Potter, Maria Olsson-Tysor, Vanessa Kanegai, and Angela Torrez, my publicists—thank you for your continued support and encouragement. I value you all beyond measure!

To Debbie Ford—you're bold and beautiful! You've unknowingly taught me more about loving who I am and accepting myself for who I am than any other human being. You constantly inspire me!

To Barbara Goodman—you're a gracious, talented, and passionate woman who's embraced me with a motherlike love and reinforced how soul supporters show up in the most unexpected places. Much love!

To Chantel Craig—what a shining star you are! I love your energy, beauty, and passion!

To Shannon Doran and Dr. Orest Jakym, my craniosacral massage therapist and chiropractor—you've separately yet synergistically freed my body of reservoirs of hidden negative energy with your magical hands. Thank you!

To Adele Fridman, my protégé in the making—stay strong and focused, and remember that you create your world. You are beautiful, intelligent, driven, and persistent, and there's nothing you can't do! I'm thrilled to have you on board with *Simply . . . Woman!* and I thank your for everything you do on the message forum.

To Kathryn Rogers—you've been such a joy to work with. From the very first session we did together, you brought as much light into my life as I did yours. Shine bright!

To Wendy Fleet—you're a magical and beautiful woman, and your gentle spirit on the message forum has been overwhelmingly powerful. Thank you for all that you do. Stay true to you!

To Jo-Anne Wade—you're *Simply . . . Woman!* Thank you for your continued support on our Website's message forum and for your loving contributions to this book. Continue to take the path of least resistance!

To Shere Donald—thank you for sharing your amazing story and for allowing your gift of healing to touch others. You are extraordinary! You are a shining light in this world.

To all the forum members of **www.crystalandrus.com**—I've never been a part of something that's as miraculous and supportive as this group. It wouldn't be what it is without you all!

To Flavio Pincente and David Hunt at Zero One Digital Communications—what amazing productions you've done for me. Thank you for believing in me from day one!

To Salim Khoja and David Sersta—The Power Within! I can't ever thank you enough for everything you've done for me.

To Dr. Simon Rego—your initial read of the original outline of this book, followed by your thought-provoking statements (and disagreements), made me "up the bar," as you unknowingly pushed me to really think about every word I was writing. Whether you agree or not with my beliefs, you helped me stretch my mind and speak *my* truth! Thank you!

To Korby Banner—photographer and makeup artist extraordinaire. Once again you've brought out the "best" in me. Thank you!

And last but certainly not least . . .

To Reid Tracy—what can I say? You've single-handedly changed my life. I will never forget the opportunities you've given me or your uncompromising support and encouragement at Hay House.

And to Louise Hay—you are, unknowingly, the voice behind most of my thoughts, discoveries, and personal breakthroughs. Your words have not only touched millions, but you've also opened up the "eyes of my eyes" and inspired me to be the woman I am! What an honor it is to be in your "family" at Hay House.

About the Author

Crystal Andrus is a passionate and powerful speaker, writer, women's advocate, and health expert, as well as the author of the best-selling book *Simply . . . Woman! The 12-Week Body-Mind-Soul Total Transformation Program.* Lecturing with top inspirational speakers such as Dr. Phil, Dr. Wayne Dyer, Louise Hay, Debbie Ford, and Dr. Christiane Northrup, she's also on faculty at the famed Omega Institute in New York.

Crystal's dedication to empowering and strengthening the spirit of women can be felt in everything she does, from her weekly radio show on Hay House Radio to her one-on-one Integrative Body-Mind-Soul Coaching and her active participation on her Website's message forum.

Certified by the American College of Sports Medicine and the Canadian School of Natural Nutrition, Crystal is working toward her Ph.D. in naturopathic medicine. A welcomed guest on television and radio shows across North America, in 2004 she was the life coach on *Canada AM*. She's also the spokesperson for the weight-loss line of health supplements, Genuine Health (**www.genuinehealth.com**).

Having grown up just outside of Toronto, Canada, Crystal now lives in a small serene town in southern Ontario with her soul mate, George; her beautiful daughters Madelaine and Julia; their golden retriever, Willow; and their flock of canaries.

Website: **www.crystalandrus.com**

Notes

Notes

Notes

We hope you enjoyed this Hay House book. If you'd like to receive a free catalog featuring additional Hay House books and products, or if you'd like information about the Hay Foundation, please contact:

Hay House, Inc.
P.O. Box 5100
Carlsbad, CA 92018-5100

(760) 431-7695 or **(800) 654-5126**
(760) 431-6948 (fax) or **(800) 650-5115 (fax)**
www.hayhouse.com® • www.hayfoundation.org

Published and distributed in Australia by:
Hay House Australia Pty. Ltd. • 18/36 Ralph St. • Alexandria NSW 2015
Phone: 612-9669-4299 • *Fax:* 612-9669-4144 • www.hayhouse.com.au

Published and distributed in the United Kingdom by:
Hay House UK, Ltd. • Unit 62, Canalot Studios
222 Kensal Rd., London W10 5BN • *Phone:* 44-20-8962-1230
Fax: 44-20-8962-1239 • www.hayhouse.co.uk

Published and distributed in the Republic of South Africa by:
Hay House SA (Pty), Ltd., P.O. Box 990, Witkoppen 2068
Phone/Fax: 27-11-706-6612 • orders@psdprom.co.za

Published in India by:
Hay House Publications (India) Pvt. Ltd., 3 Hampton Court,
A-Wing, 123 Wodehouse Rd., Colaba, Mumbai 400005
Phone: 91 (22) 22150557 or 22180533 • *Fax:* 91 (22) 22839619
www.hayhouseindia.co.in

Distributed in India by: Media Star, 7 Vaswani Mansion,
120 Dinshaw Vachha Rd., Churchgate, Mumbai 400020
Phone: 91 (22) 22815538-39-40 • *Fax:* 91 (22) 22839619
booksdivision@mediastar.co.in

Distributed in Canada by: Raincoast
9050 Shaughnessy St., Vancouver, B.C. V6P 6E5
Phone: (604) 323-7100 • *Fax:* (604) 323-2600 • www.raincoast.com

Tune in to **HayHouseRadio.com**™ for the best in inspirational talk radio featuring top Hay House authors! And, sign up via the Hay House USA Website to receive the Hay House online newsletter and stay informed about what's going on with your favorite authors. You'll receive bimonthly announcements about: Discounts and Offers, Special Events, Product Highlights, Free Excerpts, Giveaways, and more!
www.hayhouse.com®